"Wisdom That Transforms. Action That Lasts."

The Get Wisdom Commitment

At Get Wisdom Publishing we believe that true wisdom has the power to transform lives. Our mission is to equip readers with timeless insights and practical tools that inspire growth, guide decisions, and empower purposeful living. We don't just inform—we empower.

Our books combine profound understanding with real-life application, enabling readers to unlock their potential and navigate life's challenges with clarity and confidence. With each step guided by wisdom, we help you create lasting change and live the life you deserve.

When wisdom meets purpose, transformation follows.

The *OBSCURE* Bible Study Series

Grow in your faith through investigating unusual and obscure biblical characters.

"Deep Biblical Wisdom.
Real-Life Faith Application."

The OBSCURE Bible Study Journey

Meet Shamgar, Jethro, Manoah & Hathach	4 Lessons
Blasphemy, Grace, Quarrels & Reconciliation	8 Lessons
The Beginning and the End	8 Lessons
God at the Center	8 Lessons
Women of Courage	8 Lessons
The Beginning of Wisdom	8 Lessons
Miracles and Rebellion	8 Lessons
The Chosen People	8 Lessons
The Chosen Person	8 Lessons

The Chosen People

There is a remnant.

**Personal Study Guide
Book 8**

Discover the timeless lessons of the Bible!

Stephen H Berkey

GET WISDOM
PUBLISHING

COPYRIGHT

Discover the biblical characters that mainstream studies forget – and the timeless lessons they teach."

TABLE OF CONTENTS

CONTENTS

FREE PDF RESOURCES
Free PDF

Living Wisely
The Life Planning Guide

A Quick-Start Guide to Purposeful Living and Wise Decisions!

Discover the five life domains: purpose, people, principles, productivity, and perspective. Wisdom is the ability to apply truth and logic to real-life decisions and produce good outcomes. It influences your choices and will produce action that lasts. Consider and apply the five practical wisdom principles for daily living. (6 pages)

Free PDF: https://getwisdompublishing.com/resource-registration/

Living Wisely
The Life Planning Guide

Wisdom That Transforms.
Action That Lasts.

Stephen H Berkey
J.S. Wellman

Free PDF

Five Practical Principles For Life
When wisdom meets purpose, transformation follows.

Free PDF

Wise
Decision-Making

[Get the ebook version for 99 cents]

You can make good choices.

This free resource provides a project-oriented perspective and gives ten detailed steps to analyze issues/problems to determine a solution. (26 pages)

Good decisions expand your horizons. Don't allow the fear of decision-making paralyze your ability to make good choices. Think through the alternatives and move forward. When your eyes are on the goal, making good decisions is easier.

Free PDF: https://getwisdompublishing.com/resource-registration/

Kindle ebook for 99 cents: https://www.amazon.com/dp/B09SYGWRVL/

Ebook

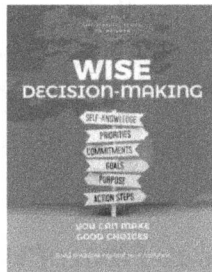

Free PDF

Make Thoughtful Decisions!

Good decisions expand your horizons.

Why Study OBSCURE Characters?

Unique, New, and Fresh
For experienced Bible students these characters will provide a fresh and interesting approach to Bible study. Since most of the material will be unfamiliar to the participants, new believers or those just starting Bible study should not feel intimidated by students who have been studying for years. Most readers will not be acquainted with the majority of the characters and events in this series.

Knowledge of Scripture
These studies are a great introduction for those just beginning Bible study. Regardless of their level of knowledge, everyone should find the characters and stories provide an opportunity to grow in their faith through investigating fascinating and unusual biblical stories and incidents.

Valuable Life Lessons
These lesser-known characters are a lot like you and me. God uses all sorts of people to accomplish His plans! You will become familiar with ordinary people, strange characters, and people living on the fringe of life who have the same troubles and challenges as people today. The deep truths and life lessons embedded in these studies should be valuable. They will provide new insights to scripture.

"Unlock Biblical Wisdom.
Transform Your faith!"

ABOUT THE LEADER GUIDE

All of the books in this Bible Study series have an extensive Leader Guide. If you are a participant in a group, a Leader Guide is not necessary, unless you want the author's answers. If you are studying independently, you may want the Leader Guide.

In the Guide the answers follow the questions with a small amount of space for the Leader's personal responses. If you are using the Leader Guide and want to do the study without the influence of the author's answers the best solution is to obtain the blank Worksheets, which are free. This will allow you to record your answers separately before reviewing the answers in the Leader Guide.

See the instructions on the previous "FREE RESOURCES" page to access the free Worksheets.

"Discover the Overlooked.
Apply it to Your Life!"

Book Description

They Were Called by God
Their Choices Still Echo Through History

Do you ever feel trapped in patterns you know are wrong, longing to break free and live a life that truly honors God? Do you desire to trust Him completely, yet find that nagging fear keeps holding you back?

This book invites you to explore the lives of those specifically chosen by God, some celebrated and some obscure. You will discover how their choices continue to impact us today. Through focused biblical wisdom this study will equip you to understand God's overarching plan and empower you to live with unwavering faith, no matter the circumstances.

Delve into the heart of Lucifer, Michael the Archangel, and Job's Wife. You will find lessons that can be used today. Learn to trust God in every situation, regardless of circumstances.

This isn't just a history lesson; it's a guide to building an unshakable faith, making wise choices, and understanding God's purpose for your life. Are you ready to challenge your faith and grow closer to God?

Book 8 is about the chosen people. It might be considered an introduction to Book 9, which is about the chosen person – Jesus. The book begins with two lessons about angels – first Lucifer (the devil) and second, the archangel Michael.

Lucifer is referred to by a number of names, the most common being Satan. If we have a better understanding of the nature of evil we should have a better chance of overcoming Satan's temptations. This is no small task as Paul tells us that we need to put on the full armor of God in order to stand against the devil's schemes.

Job's wife is the subject after Michael the archangel and the focus is on the Retribution Principle, which states that if a person is righteous, he will prosper and if a person is wicked, he will suffer.

The lesson on Achan introduces us to the concept of "devoted things" and we gain a unique understanding of spiritual gifts as we study how God grants special knowledge to Bezalel and Oholiab so they could make and construct the Tabernacle.

The next lesson is about Jeduthun who was chosen by king David to lead worship and give thanks to the Lord when the Ark of the Covenant was returned to the temple.

In ancient days the watchman was responsible for warning the people of danger and the prophet's role as a watchman was to warn Israel of their rebellion and call them to repentance. The watchman prophets carried out their responsibilities but their message fell on deaf ears. The shepherd leaders of Israel had failed. They led the people into idolatry and rebellion.

Lastly, Book 8 examines Isaiah's son Shear-Jashub. God's people were living an illusion because of the absence of justice, faithfulness, and righteousness. Isaiah was called as a prophet and his message was one of doom if the people would not repent. The one glimmer of hope was Shear-Jashub, whose name means "a remnant will return."

"Scripture holds answers in unexpected places. Our unique Bible studies reveal overlooked wisdom for today's challenges."

INTRODUCTION

*We equip readers with timeless wisdom and practical tools
that transform, not just inform. Our books combine
deep insights with real-life application
to create lasting change.*

Description of The OBSCURE Bible Study Series

This unique series uses a number of lesser-known Bible characters
and events to explore such major themes as Angels, being Born
Again, Courage, Death, Evangelism, Faithfulness, Forgiveness,
Grace, Hell, Leadership, Miracles, the Remnant, the Sabbath,
Salvation, Rebellion, Sovereignty, Thankfulness, Women, the
World, Creation, and End Times.

The series as a whole provides both a broad and fresh
understanding of the nature of God as we see Him act in the lives
of people we've never examined before.

Most of the people chosen for these studies are unfamiliar because
they are mentioned only a few times in Scripture – fifteen only
once or twice. Others, although more familiar, are included
because of their particular contribution to kingdom work.

For example, Scripture mentions Shamgar only twice. One verse in
Judges 3:31 tells his story and 5:6 simply establishes a timeline and
says nothing more about him. Then there is Nicodemus, with
whom we associate the concept of being "born again." His name
appears only 5 times, all in one short passage in the book of John.
Eve, although obviously not obscure, is included in order to
investigate the creation story.

Group Discussion or Individual Study

These studies can be done individually or in a small discussion
group. The real value of the study is in the discussion questions.
We all see life differently and the thoughts and ideas shared in a

group will often lead to a richer understanding of the Scripture. The questions often require the participant to put himself (herself) in the mind or circumstances of that person in the Scriptures.

The commentary portion of the introductory material in each lesson is there to help clarify the passage and set the stage for the discussion questions. The questions are designed to help the student understand the meaning of the text itself and explore the kingdom implications from a personal point of view.

Ideal For Both New and Mature Bible Students

These lessons have three underlying questions:

- "Who is this person?"
- "What is happening here?"
- "What is the implication for my life?"

Because of the obscurity of the characters under study, chances are that even experienced participants with prior understanding of the lesson's theme will find fresh material to explore. Both new and long-time students will be challenged by the life lessons these unfamiliar characters can teach them.

Format of Lessons

Each lesson begins with the Scripture using the ESV translation followed by short sections titled "Context," "What Do We Know," and "Observations." The discussion questions are designed to help the student understand the subject and are followed by several application questions.

"We believe applied wisdom empowers life change. Our books provide clarity, inspiration, and tools to equip readers to live their best life."

Lucifer
the Devil

Occurrences of "Lucifer" in the Bible: 1

Theme: Satan

Scripture

Isa 14:12   The Fall of Lucifer

*"How you are fallen from heaven, O **Lucifer**, son of the morning! How you are cut down to the ground, You who weakened the nations!"* NKJV

John 13:21-27

*. . . "Truly, truly, I say to you, one of you will betray me." 22 The disciples looked at one another, uncertain of whom he spoke. . . . 25 So that disciple, leaning back against Jesus, said to him, "Lord, who is it?" 26 Jesus answered, "It is he to whom I will give this morsel of bread when I have dipped it." So when he had dipped the morsel, he gave it to Judas, the son of Simon Iscariot. 27 Then after he had taken the morsel, **Satan** entered into him. Jesus said to him, "What you are going to do, do quickly."* ESV

The Context

Satan (the Devil) is referred to by multiple names throughout Scripture about 100-120 times, but the name for Satan, *Lucifer*, is only found once. The most frequent used names for Lucifer in the Bible are:

Satan	52
Devil	30
Evil One	12
Serpent	9

Lucifer and Judas are an interesting and unique combination in the Bible because John 13:27 says, "*After Judas ate the piece of bread, Satan entered him*. . . *.*" Judas Iscariot was one of the Twelve chosen by Jesus to be an Apostle. Why would Jesus choose someone He knew would betray Him? Wouldn't it have been better to have another faithful Apostle and permit someone outside the small group of followers to be the betrayer?

What Do We Know?

To gain a sense of the relative importance of Satan in the Bible, note that Peter is mentioned 155 times in the New Testament and Satan is referred to 100-120 times. Satan is referred to in some way in more than half the books in the New Testament. Jesus talked about him and was tempted by him in the desert before He started His ministry. Satan is real!

Paul spoke about Satan:

Ephesians 6:12   *For we do not wrestle against flesh and blood, but against the rulers, against the authorities, against the cosmic powers over this present darkness, against the spiritual forces of evil in the heavenly places.* ESV

Paul introduced this subject in Eph 6:10-11 when he said that we are to be strong and we should put on the full armor of God "*so that [we] can take our stand against the devil's schemes.*"

Implications and Observations

What is the nature of evil and Satan? If we have a better understanding of the nature of evil and how to fight or resist it, then we should have a better chance of being overcomers. Some think that experiencing temptation is in itself a sin. That is not true. The sin is in acting on temptation or evil desires. It's similar to an alcoholic going into a bar and drinking soda while his friends consume something stronger. He is not in trouble until he actually takes a drink.

But it is not wise to push the envelope like this – in fact it may be downright foolish and stupid. If you don't want to be tempted by pornography then don't buy dirty magazines in order to read the "wonderful articles." If you don't want to be tempted by the opposite sex, then avoid being alone with them. If you don't want to be tempted by money and power, give it away or allow someone else to have authority over it. If you don't want to be tempted by drugs and alcohol, choose friends who will not encourage their use. It is really not that difficult to take basic steps to shield yourself from temptation. The hard thing is believing it is necessary.

We all need to be asking for God's protection from temptation, desire, and sin. God will help but we have some responsibility to make wise choices about where we go, what we do, and who we spend time with. But sometimes even the best laid plans of men go astray. Joseph refused the advances of Potifar's wife on many occasions, but he still landed in prison although he did nothing wrong. God was ultimately faithful, but lesser men would have given up on God. So what do we do?

- Stay away, run away, avoid, and flee from dangerous situations.

- Resist through the power of God's Word.

- Pray for protection (1 Cor 10:13).

- Put on the full armor of God (Eph 6).

- Set your mind on things above, positive things, and godly things (Php 4:8; Ro 8:5).

- Do not love the world, be a friend to the world, or conform to the world (James 4:4; Romans 12:2; 1 John 2:15).

- Enlist an accountability partner.

Discussion Questions

In the 1960-70s a comedian named Flip Wilson made famous the phrase, "The devil made me do it." Is this good theology? No, Satan cannot make us do anything, unless we let him. He can tempt us, encourage us, and trick us, but he cannot force us. We have free will to make a choice. Ultimately we decide.

A. HISTORY OF THE ENEMY

A1. We are going to look at two passages in the Old Testament that have dual meanings or "double fulfillment." This means that they apply to two different situations, usually one in the present or near future and another much later time. The first is a passage in Isaiah that applied to the King of Babylon, but also describes our enemy, Satan:

> Isaiah 14:9-15   *Sheol beneath is stirred up to meet you when you come; it rouses the shades to greet you, all who were leaders of the earth; it raises from their thrones all who were kings of the nations. 10 All of them will answer and say to you: 'You too have become as weak as we! You have become like us!' 11 Your pomp is brought down to Sheol, the sound of your harps; maggots are laid as a bed beneath you, and worms are your covers. 12 "How you are fallen from heaven, O Day Star, son of Dawn! How you are cut down to the ground, you who laid the nations low! 13 You said in your heart, 'I will ascend to heaven; above the stars of God I will set my throne on high; I will sit on the mount of assembly in the far reaches of the north; 14 I will ascend above the heights of the clouds; I will make myself like the Most High.' 15 But you are brought down to Sheol, to the far reaches of the pit. ESV*

Q. Lucifer made five "I will" statements in Isa 14:13-14. What are they?

I will _____.

I will _____.

I will _____.

I will _____.

I will _____.

Q. What sin would summarize these statements?

A2. A second Old Testament passage also involves a double fulfillment prophecy that in that day concerned the King of Tyre:

> Ezekiel 28:12-19   *"Son of man, raise a lamentation over the king of Tyre, and say to him, Thus says the Lord God:*
>
> *You were the signet of perfection, full of wisdom and perfect in beauty.13 You were in Eden, the garden of God; every precious stone was your covering, sardius, topaz, and diamond, beryl, onyx, and jasper, sapphire, emerald, and carbuncle; and crafted in gold were your settings and your engravings. On the day that you were created they were prepared.14 You were an anointed guardian cherub. I placed you; you were on the holy mountain of God; in the midst of the stones of fire you walked.15 You were blameless in your ways from the day you were created, till unrighteousness was found in you.16 In the abundance of your trade you were filled with violence in your midst, and you sinned; so I cast you as a profane thing from the mountain of God, and I destroyed you, O guardian cherub, from the midst of the stones of fire. 17 Your heart was proud because of your beauty; you corrupted your wisdom for the sake of your splendor. I cast you to the ground; I*

exposed you before kings, to feast their eyes on you.18 By the multitude of your iniquities, in the unrighteousness of your trade you profaned your sanctuaries; so I brought fire out from your midst; it consumed you, and I turned you to ashes on the earth in the sight of all who saw you.19 All who know you among the peoples are appalled at you; you have come to a dreadful end and shall be no more forever." ESV

Lucifer is referred to here as a "cherub." These creatures are generally associated with the praise and worship of God. You may remember they were assigned in Genesis 3 to guard the Garden of Eden so that no one could have access to the tree of life.

Q.   What were the reasons Lucifer fell from grace?

28:15 _____ .

28:16 _____ and _____.

28:17a _____.

28:17b _____.

28:18 _____,

A3. The Book of Revelation describes the great dragon (Satan) being thrown out of heaven:

Revelation 12:9-10   *And the great dragon was thrown down, that ancient serpent, who is called the devil and Satan, the deceiver of the whole world— he was thrown down to the earth, and his angels were thrown down with him. 10 And I heard a loud voice in heaven, saying, "Now the salvation and the power and the kingdom of our God and the authority of his Christ have come, for the accuser of our brothers has been thrown down, who accuses them day and night before our God.* ESV

Q. What is the sin of Satan described in 12:9 and what does it mean?

Q. What does Satan do (12:10) and what does it mean?

A4. The New Testament reports that the spirit of Satan is still alive and well. He will be there at the end still trying to exalt himself above God:

2 Thessalonians 2:3-5   *Let no one deceive you in any way. For that day will not come, unless the rebellion comes first, and the man of lawlessness is revealed, the son of destruction, 4 who opposes and exalts himself against every so-called god or object of worship, so that he takes his seat in the temple of God, proclaiming himself to be God. 5 Do you not remember that when I was still with you I told you these things?* ESV

Q. What sins, listed in 2:4 above, describe the nature of Satan?

B. SATAN IN THE GARDEN

We first encounter Satan in the early pages of the Book of Genesis where he is disguised as a serpent or snake: Genesis 3:1 *Now the serpent was the most cunning of all the wild animals that the Lord God had made. He said to the woman, "Did God really say, 'You can't eat from any tree in the garden?'"*

B1. From just this one verse, what can you conclude about Satan?

    a. His nature: _____.

    b. His talk: _____.

    c. His lies: _____.

B2. What does Satan do in Gen 3:4-5?
Genesis 3:4-5   *But the serpent said to the woman, "You will not surely die. 5 For God knows that when you eat of it your eyes will be opened, and you will be like God, knowing good and evil." ESV*

B3. In Gen 3:8-10 what did Adam and Eve do and what does it mean?
Genesis 3:8-10   *And they heard the sound of the Lord God walking in the garden in the cool of the day, and the man and his wife hid themselves from the presence of the Lord God among the trees of the garden. 9 But the Lord God called to the man and said to him, "Where are you?" 10 And he said, "I heard the sound of you in the garden, and I was afraid, because I was naked, and I hid myself." ESV*

B4. What else can we learn about Satan from Genesis 3:11-13?
He said, "Who told you that you were naked? Have you eaten of the tree of which I commanded you not to eat?" 12 The man said, "The woman whom you gave to be with me, she gave me fruit of the tree, and I ate." 13 Then the Lord God said to the woman, "What is this that you have done?" The woman said, "The serpent deceived me, and I ate." ESV

Q. Who lied?

Q. Who does Adam blame in Gen 3:12?

Q. Who does Eve blame in Gen 3:13?

C. NATURE OF SATAN

C1. Judas had already gone to the Chief Priest and made arrangements for the betrayal before Satan entered Judas. Satan did not cause or force Judas to be a traitor before the kiss in the garden. Judas had already decided he was going to turn Jesus over to the authorities. If that is true then why did Satan enter Judas?

C2. When do you find yourself most vulnerable to Satan?

C3. Satan twists God's words. When Jesus was tempted in the desert Satan misused and misquoted God's word. Satan did the same thing in the Garden. Therefore we must be very diligent in knowing and understanding the Word of God:

> a. We must be _____ about what Scripture says, even when it is challenging.
> b. Our interpretation must be _____ with all Scripture. It must be in harmony with the entirety of God's Word.
> c. We must not take Scripture out of _____. It must agree with the historical meaning.

C4. How does James 4:7 say we are to deal with the devil/evil? James 4:7   *Submit yourselves therefore to God. Resist the devil, and he will flee from you.* ESV (see also Eph 4:27; 6:11; 1Pet 5:8-9)

C5. Why would Satan want to tempt someone who is already a Christian?
> 1. Destroy their _____ with God/Jesus.
> 2. Destroy their _____ in and dependence on God.
> 3. Destroy their_____.
> 4. Make them question their _____ in Christ.
> 5. Shake their _____ in the Bible.

C6. Which of the following statements are true?

(a) "If I'm a Christian and live right, I'll automatically be covered against Satan's attacks." True/False? _____.

(b) "You don't know how intense my temptations are! I just can't handle them. They overpower me." True/False? _____.

(c) "Why flee my temptations? I can survive, and I like the thrill of 'standing on the edge'." True/False? _____.

(d) "I don't really believe all that occult stuff about Satan and spiritual opposition." True/False? _____.

(e) "Why start over when you know you'll fail again? I think some sins are just meant to be part of us." True/False? _____.

D. NAMES (or descriptions) OF SATAN

D1. Following are names of or descriptions of the character of Satan. Define or expand the meaning of the name.

   (A) 2 Thess 2:3-4
   Man of Lawlessness; Son of Destruction.

(B) Matt 4:3-4
Tempter.

    Q. In what areas of life does Satan often tempt people?

(C) Rev 12:9-10
Great Dragon; Devil; Deceiver.

(D) 2 Cor 4:4
God of this world.

(E) 1 John 5:18-19
Evil One.

    Q. How can Satan be the god of this world? I
    thought God was in charge?

(F) Isaiah 14:12
Morning star.
Destroyer of nations.

(G) 1 Peter 5:8
Adversary.

(H) John 8:44
Devil; Murderer; Father of Liars.

(I) Revelation 12:10-11
Accuser.

(J) 2 Corinthians 11:14
Angel of light.

D2. Write a short summary or list of what you conclude from the answers to D1 above:

_____
_____
_____
_____
_____
_____
_____
_____
_____
_____

E. APPLICATION

E1. Do you believe Lucifer is real? Why? Why not?
What evidence do you have to support your position?

E2. Do you pray against the spiritual forces of evil? Why? Why not?

Michael
the archangel

Occurrences of "Michael" in the Bible: 5

NOTE: The words "angel" or "angels" appear in the Bible 295 times.

Theme: Angels

Scripture

Dan 10:10-21

And behold, a hand touched me and set me trembling on my hands and knees. 11 And he said to me, "O Daniel, man greatly loved, understand the words that I speak to you, and stand upright, for now I have been sent to you." And when he had spoken this word to me, I stood up trembling. 12 Then he said to me, "Fear not, Daniel, for from the first day that you set your heart to understand and humbled yourself before your God, your words have been heard, and I have come because of your words. 13 The prince of the kingdom of Persia withstood me twenty-one days, but Michael, one of the chief princes, came to help me, for I was left there with the kings of Persia, 14 and came to make you understand what is to happen to your people in the latter days. For the vision is for days yet to come."

15 When he had spoken to me according to these words, I turned my face toward the ground and was mute. 16 And behold, one in the likeness of the children of man touched my lips. Then I opened my mouth and spoke. I said to him who stood before me, "O my lord, by reason of the vision pains have come upon me, and I retain no strength. 17 How can my lord's servant talk with my lord? For now no strength remains in me, and no breath is left in me."

18 Again one having the appearance of a man touched me and strengthened me. 19 And he said, "O man greatly loved, fear not, peace be with you; be strong and of good courage." And as he spoke to me, I was strengthened and said, "Let my lord speak, for you have strengthened me." 20 Then he said, "Do you know why I have come to you? But now I will return to fight against the prince of Persia; and when I go out, behold, the prince of Greece will come. 21 But I will tell you what is inscribed in the book of truth: there is none who contends by my side against these except Michael, your prince. ESV

Dan 12:1
At that time shall arise Michael, the great prince who has charge of your people. And there shall be a time of trouble, such as never has been since there was a nation till that time. But at that time your people shall be delivered, everyone whose name shall be found written in the book. ESV

Jude 9-10
But when the archangel Michael, contending with the devil, was disputing about the body of Moses, he did not presume to pronounce a blasphemous judgment, but said, "The Lord rebuke you." 10 But these people blaspheme all that they do not understand, and they are destroyed by all that they, like unreasoning animals, understand instinctively. ESV

Rev 12:7-9
Now war arose in heaven, Michael and his angels fighting against the dragon. And the dragon and his angels fought back, 8 but he was defeated and there was no longer any place for them in heaven. 9 And the great dragon was thrown down, that ancient serpent, who is called the devil and Satan, the deceiver of the whole world — he was thrown down to the earth, and his angels were thrown down with him. ESV

The Context

Although angels are mentioned throughout scripture, we actually know relatively little about them. By definition, they are "divine messengers." These spiritual beings were created to serve God in various ways, but some rebelled with Satan and were thrown out of heaven.

We can assume the angels were created by Jesus because scripture tells us that "by Him all things were created, both in the heavens and on earth" (Col 1:16). It does not, however, tell us exactly when they were created, nor does it give us a full understanding of their purpose and function.

The Bible describes several categories of angels, among which are cherubim and seraphim. Another special angel is "the Angel of the Lord," who is often considered a manifestation of God Himself, or the pre-incarnate Christ.

In addition, two angels are mentioned by name: Gabriel (Dan 8:16; 9:21; Luke 1:19, 26) and Michael, the archangel (Jude 9). Some consider the "star of the morning" mentioned in Isaiah 14:12 to be Satan, and some translations translate this phrase as "Lucifer."

Angels in the Gospels

Jesus mentioned angels on a number of occasions in the Gospels:

1) Angels are involved in the harvest at the end of the age (Mt 13:39-41).

2) We have personal angels. Nothing in the Bible says specifically that each of the Elect has a personal guardian angel. But the personal pronoun "their" in Mt 18:10 certainly is a strong hint that there may be some kind of association. For example in Heb 1:14 and Ps 91:11 we see that the angels have responsibilities for us in some way.
3) Matthew 25:31 indicates angels will be with Jesus when He comes to reign (see also Mk 8:38, 13:27; Mt 13:39-41, and 16:27).

In Rev 19:14 it says the armies of heaven followed Him on white horses. This is most likely the "vast multitude" and "heaven dwellers" referred to elsewhere. Thus, although referred to as an army they are probably not the angel armies.

In Rev 17:14 it says that those with him are the "called, chosen, and faithful." Although the angels return with Him, it is not the angels being referenced in 19:14, but rather the Elect. Angels are never referenced in this manner but the Elect are, so these must be the believers returning with Christ. But in Mt 26:53, it indicates Jesus could call on "legions of angels."

4) Luke 12:8-9 indicates angels are involved or part of the power structure in heaven.

5) Angels know what is happening on the earth (Lk 15:10). Paul also makes reference to angels knowing or seeing the actions of men (1 Cor 4:9).

6) Angels are described as holy in Mark 8:38.

7) Angels were the first to sin. Adam was the first of the human race to sin after "Creation." Eve was tempted by the serpent (Devil) to sin but he and his angels had already sinned.
(Gen 3:1-7, 14-15; Rev 12:7-9; 2 Pet 2:4; Isa 14:12-15; Ezk 28:11-17)

8) Do humans become angels when they die? No! It may be great in the movies but it is not scriptural.

9) Should angels be worshipped or prayed to? Absolutely not! Only God is to be worshipped (Rev 19:10).

Cherubim

Angels in God's presence include the cherubim, seraphim, and living creatures (or living beings):

> Ex 25:20   The **cherubim** shall spread out their wings above, overshadowing the mercy seat with their wings,

their faces one to another; toward the mercy seat shall the faces of the cherubim be. ESV

Isa 6:2   *Above him stood the **seraphim**. Each had six wings: with two he covered his face, and with two he covered his feet, and with two he flew. ESV*

Rev 4:6   *and before the throne there was as it were a sea of glass, like crystal. And around the throne, on each side of the throne, are four **living creatures**, full of eyes in front and behind* (ESV).
NOTE: Ezekiel 1:5-6 also refers to living creatures that had human form.

Cherubim are mentioned 65 times in the Bible. They are a special category of angel or heavenly host and seem to be higher than "regular" angels. Satan was apparently in this special category of angel as he is referred to as a "guardian cherub." (Eze 28:14-16)

In Genesis 3:24 we learn that cherubim have a very unique responsibility in that they guard the tree of life in the Garden of Eden. This responsibility for guarding is also seen in 1 Kings 6:23-29.

Seraphim

Seraphim are only mentioned twice in the Bible and again seem to be a special kind of angel similar to the cherubim described above. In Isaiah 6:2-6 the seraphim are standing around the throne of God. They are worshipping God, saying "Holy. Holy, Holy. . ." They also are serving God and carrying out His instructions.

What Else Do We Know?

God's angels are often seen in heaven or they are coming from heaven. This probably implies that heaven is their home or base of operations. We know from the book of Revelation that there are many angels or heavenly beings around the throne of God. How much time they spend on earth or in heaven is unknown.

Fallen angels probably are not allowed in heaven since sin cannot be in the presence of God. When Lucifer ("star of the morning" Isaiah 14:12) and his rebel angels lost their status in heaven they were sent out of the presence of God. We can assume that the demons mentioned in the Bible are part of the group of "angels and heavenly beings" that revolted against God. Lucifer, known as Satan or the Devil, is identified as the leader of the rebellion. Only one other fallen angel is identified in Scripture: Abaddon or Apollyon (Rev 9:11), "the angel of the bottomless pit" (or abyss).

Angels always appear to God's people, never to evil or wicked people. They appeared to Abraham, David, Daniel, Jesus and many more. Their appearance often caused fear and in fact, their first words were often, "Do not be afraid." Most of us remember the angel's words to the shepherds in the fields when he brought the news of Jesus' birth (Lk 2:8-14). Their appearance is also often described as very exciting or dazzling: *"While they were perplexed about this, suddenly two men stood by them in dazzling clothes."* (Luke 24:4)

Discussion Questions

A. ANGELS.

A1. In Mark 8:38 the angels are called holy. Yet we know that Lucifer and about a third of the angels who followed Lucifer rebelled against God. How can we harmonize this apparent contradiction? [see Mt 25:41 and 1 Tim 5:21]

A2. DEFINITION: Find and record a short definition or description of an angel:

A3. Hebrews 1:14 *Are they not all ministering spirits sent out to serve for the sake of those who are to inherit salvation?* ESV

a) What does "ministering spirits" mean?

b) Who do they serve?

c) What do they do?

A4. Angels are described in Hebrews and by Peter:
Hebrews 2:7 *You made him for a little while lower than the angels; you have crowned him with glory and honor,* ESV
2 Peter 2:11 *whereas angels, though greater in might and power, do not pronounce a blasphemous judgment against them before the Lord.* ESV

a) What does it mean that men are "lower than the angels"?

b) Is that relationship between man and angels going to change?

c) What does it mean that angels are "greater in might and power"?

d) Can you think of examples when angels demonstrated their superior strength and powers?

A5. What are the angels doing in the following verses? What is their function?

a) Angels give God _____.
Ps 148:1-2   *Praise the Lord! Praise the Lord from the heavens; praise him in the heights! 2 Praise him, all his angels; praise him, all his hosts!* ESV

b) Large numbers are *at* _____.
1 Kings 22:19   *Therefore hear the word of the Lord: I saw the Lord sitting on his throne, and all the host of heaven standing beside him on his right hand and on his left;* ESV

c) Angels give _____.
Matt 2:13   *Now when they had departed, behold, an angel of the Lord appeared to Joseph in a dream and said, "Rise, take the child and his mother, and flee to Egypt, and remain there until I tell you, for Herod is about to search for the child, to destroy him."* ESV

d) Angels bring God's _____.
2 Sam 24:16   *And when the angel stretched out his hand toward Jerusalem to destroy it, the Lord relented from the calamity and said to the angel who was working destruction among the people, "It is enough; now stay your hand." . . .* ESV

e) Angels are used to help God's people in times of _____.
Hebrews 1:14   *Are they not all ministering spirits sent out to serve for the sake of those who are to inherit salvation?* ESV

f) Angels appear in _____ to give guidance or help to God's people.
Gen 31:11   *Then the angel of God said to me in the dream, 'Jacob,' and I said, 'Here I am!'* ESV

g) Angels _____ God's people.
Daniel 3:28   *Nebuchadnezzar answered and said, "Blessed be the God of Shadrach, Meshach, and Abednego, who has sent his angel and delivered his servants, who trusted in him, . . ."* ESV

h) Angels deliver God's people from _____.
Acts 5:19   *But during the night an angel of the Lord opened the prison doors and brought them out, and said . . ."* ESV

i) Angels ministered to Jesus during His ministry on earth (Mark 1:13; Luke 22:43).

j) Angels bring answers to prayer (Acts 12:5-10).

k) Angels often appear in human form (Gen 18:2; Dan 10:18).

l) Three angels make the final proclamations at the end of time (Revelation 14:6-12).

A6. Do you find the idea of angels scary, comforting, weird, attractive . . . what? Why?

A7. Do angels have free will?

B. MICHAEL and the ANGELS:

B1. Why did the angel come in Dan 10:12?

Q. When does it say Daniel's prayers were heard?

B2. What can you conclude about angels from Dan 10:13?

B3. What is the angel going to do for Daniel in 10:14?

B4. Daniel 12:1-2   *At that time shall arise Michael, the great prince who has charge of your people. And there shall be a time of trouble, such as never has been since there was a nation till that time. But at that time your people shall be delivered, everyone whose name shall be found written in the book. 2 And many of those who sleep in the dust of the earth shall awake, some to everlasting life, and some to shame and everlasting contempt.* ESV

Q. What do we learn about the Jews in Dan 12:1-2?

B5. What do we learn about Michael's status in Jude 9?

Jude 9   *But when the archangel Michael, contending with the devil, was disputing about the body of Moses, he did not presume to pronounce a blasphemous judgment, but said, "The Lord rebuke you." ESV*

B6. What do we learn about Michael's authority in Jude 9?

E. APPLICATION

E1. Have you ever had any kind of interaction with what you concluded was an angel? Explain.

E2. Do you know anyone who claims to have had an experience with an angel? Explain.

E3. Have you read historical accounts of the appearance of angels? Explain.

Wife
of Job

Occurrences of "wife (of Job)" in the Bible: 3
plus two pronouns

Themes: Retribution Principle; Rejecting God

Scripture

Job 2:6-10
And the Lord said to Satan, "Behold, he is in your hand; only spare his life." 7 So Satan went out from the presence of the Lord and struck Job with loathsome sores from the sole of his foot to the crown of his head. 8 And he took a piece of broken pottery with which to scrape himself while he sat in the ashes. 9 Then his wife said to him, "Do you still hold fast your integrity? Curse God and die." 10 But he said to her, "You speak as one of the foolish women would speak. Shall we receive good from God, and shall we not receive evil?" In all this Job did not sin with his lips. ESV

Job 19:16-19
I call to my servant, but he gives me no answer; I must plead with him with my mouth for mercy. 17 My breath is strange to my wife, and I am a stench to the children of my own mother. 18 Even young children despise me; when I rise they talk against me. 19 All my intimate friends abhor me, and those whom I loved have turned against me. ESV

Job 31:7-10
if my step has turned aside from the way and my heart has gone after my eyes, and if any spot has stuck to my hands, 8 then let me sow, and another eat, and let what grows for me be rooted out. 9 "If my heart has been enticed toward a woman, and I have lain in wait at my neighbor's door, 10 then let my wife grind for another, and let others bow down on her." ESV

Wisdom Literature

The book of Job is considered wisdom literature and by definition that means it makes frequent use of hypothetical situations and designed dialogue. Therefore, there is no reason to overemphasize the historicity of the specific conversations in Job. There is also no real reason to doubt that the narrative is based on the experience of real people. Once one recognizes the underlying theological message of the book, the questions of time, place, and history are of relatively little importance.

Overview of the Book of Job

Chapters 1-2:
Job 1:8-11   Then the Lord said to Satan, "Have you considered My servant Job? No one else on earth is like him, a man of perfect integrity, who fears God and turns away from evil." 9 Satan answered the Lord, "Does Job fear God for nothing? 10 Haven't You placed a hedge around him, his household, and everything he owns? You have blessed the work of his hands, and his possessions are spread out in the land. 11 But stretch out Your hand and strike everything he owns, and he will surely curse You to Your face."

Satan then caused Job to lose his family, his wealth, and his health, but Job did not blame God. Job's wife, however, was not as understanding.

Chapters 3-37:

Job argued with his friends about why he was suffering. His friends argued that Job's suffering was caused by sin and if Job would admit that sin and repent he would get right with God. Although Job agreed with the general concept, he claimed innocence and "demanded" that God give him an audience so he could present his case to God.

Chapters 38-end

Finally God spoke to Job and said, "*Who is this who obscures My counsel with ignorant words? . . . Will the one who contends with the Almighty correct Him? Let him who argues with God give an answer. . . . Would you really challenge My justice? Would you declare Me guilty to justify yourself?. . . everything under heaven belongs to Me.*" ESV

Job concluded by saying, "*I know that You can do anything and no plan of Yours can be thwarted. 3 You asked, Who is this who conceals My counsel with ignorance? Surely I spoke about things I did not understand, things too wonderful for me to know. . . . 6 Therefore I take back my words and repent in dust and ashes.*" (Job 42:2-3, 6 ESV)

Job did not have all the information necessary to understand the nature or cause of his suffering. He had agonized over his circumstances with a sincere heart, but he had not discerned the plan and purposes of God.

Retribution Principle

The Retribution Principle states that if a person is righteous, he will prosper and if a person is wicked, he will suffer. The corollary of this principle is that if a person prospered, he must be righteous, and if a person suffered, he must be wicked. There are a number of proverbs that illustrate this concept: if you do good you will receive blessing, but if you act badly, then terrible results occur.

This principle was widely accepted by Israel and many other cultures. People wanted a logical explanation for suffering and the Retribution Principle seemed to be the perfect answer. But, the theory and the experience did not always harmonize. Although this seemed like a logical explanation, it caused great consternation in actual human experience because in real life, there were godly righteous people who were suffering severely and unrighteous people who were not suffering.

Theodicy [thee AUD uh see]:

Theodicy is the *defense of God's goodness and omnipotence in view of the existence of evil.* The issue is understood best as a question: How can the justice of an almighty God be defended in the face of evil, especially human suffering and particularly the suffering of the innocent?

This is likely the overall purpose of the book of Job, and it raises two primary questions:

> (1) Is God right about the "righteousness" of Job? Or, is Satan correct that Job is really not upright and blameless, and not a man of integrity. Is Job only going along because God is blessing him? These challenges of Satan called into question the very plan and policies of God.

> (2) How do we explain and understand the suffering of Job – someone who is innocent, but yet suffers greatly?

Job's friends affirmed the deduced Corollary to be true and although they never presented any Scriptural arguments, Israelites in general believed it to be true. Thus, it was the basis for the friends' accusations against Job. If the Principle and the Corollary are true, and if God is just, then Job must be guilty of some terrible sin(s). And that is illustrated, evident, or proven by the extent of Job's suffering.

But in the face of this belief system, Job insisted he was innocent and did not deserve such suffering and thus looked upon God's justice with some degree of suspicion! And there is the crux of the problem – belief and reality don't match up.

God's stated view of Job occurs in 1:8 where He says, *"Have you considered My servant Job? No one else on earth is like him, a man of perfect integrity, who fears God and turns away from evil."* Thus,

if Satan can demonstrate that God is wrong, then Satan has "proven" that God's redemption plan for man is flawed. Therefore, the separation between God and man can never be bridged – making redemption unthinkable. God's policies were being put on trial by Satan, and God allowed Job's righteousness to be tested.

Conclusion

The adversary is ultimately silenced! Satan is not mentioned again after Chapter 2. The message for those people who suffer is that God's righteousness has such supreme value that God treasures it above all things. Thus, the suffering of the righteous has great meaning and value, but the cause of human suffering cannot be accurately determined and no one has sufficient wisdom to call God's justice into question. Human suffering can cause even the strongest believers to doubt the reality of God's love and power. Believers fall into the trap of thinking that somehow God's love and power are overcome or insufficient in the light of such suffering.

Skeptics point to human suffering in an attempt to justify unbelief. Some believers who experience suffering have abandoned the church, stopped praying, or become active cynics. The message of Job is that God wants His people to maintain their trust in Him, even when life is difficult and things go wrong. Anyone can believe and trust if every day is Christmas and life is good.

Discussion Questions

A. GENERAL

A1. Did Job and his wife have any direct reason to believe that Satan or God were involved with Job's suffering?

A2. Based on 2:8 what do you conclude about the nature of the sickness(s) inflicted on Job? Why?

A3. Job was apparently sitting in ashes (2:8). What does that mean or imply?

A4. Other than great suffering, what other meaning might be associated with Job sitting in ashes [see also 42:6]?

A5. Apparently while Job was sitting in pain among the ashes his wife came to him and asked a question, but before receiving any answer she told him what to do. What is the question?

QUESTION: _____.

Q. What is implied by the word _still_?

Q. What do you think the wife meant by *integrity*?

A6. What was the wife's advice or instruction to her husband?

ADVICE: _____.

A7. What multiple sins was the wife suggesting Job should incur?

Q. If Job was in fact guilty, is this the proper response?

A8. Why do you think the wife said these things?

A9. How seriously do you view the wife's comments in light of Lev 24:10-16?

Now an Israelite woman's son, whose father was an Egyptian, went out among the people of Israel. And the Israelite woman's son and a man of Israel fought in the camp, 11 and the Israelite woman's son blasphemed the Name, and cursed. Then they brought him to Moses. His mother's name was Shelomith, the daughter of Dibri, of the tribe of Dan. 12 And they put him in custody, till the will of the

Lord should be clear to them. 13 Then the Lord spoke to Moses, saying, 14 "Bring out of the camp the one who cursed, and let all who heard him lay their hands on his head, and let all the congregation stone him. 15 And speak to the people of Israel, saying, whoever curses his God shall bear his sin. 16 Whoever blasphemes the name of the Lord shall surely be put to death. All the congregation shall stone him. The sojourner as well as the native, when he blasphemes the Name, shall be put to death. ESV

A10. Do you think the punishment in Lev 24 above was appropriate?

A11. What is your general reaction to the wife's attitude?

A12. What do you think the wife should have done or said, given her situation?

A13. If Satan was the influence behind the wife's words, why would Job's death accomplish results Satan wants?

A14. Job then said, "*Should we accept only good from God and not adversity?*" What do <u>you</u> think Job meant by this?

A15. Do you think Job viewed his condition as punishment for sin?

A16. What are the possible ways Job may have been thinking about his condition at this time?

A17. What impact did Job's wife have on Job?

A18. Job 19:16-19 describes a number of situations where Job was rejected. What are they?

Q. How would you feel and respond to a situation like this?

FEEL: _____.

RESPOND: _____.

A19. In Chapter 31 Job listed a number of sins and particularly sins of the heart. In 31:9-12 he addressed marital infidelity. Job mentioned his wife again! Do you think there is any significance to mentioning the wife or is it just an attempt to illustrate how innocent Job thought he was?

Job 31:10   *then let my wife grind for another, and let others bow down on her.* ESV

B. APPLICATION

B1. <u>WOMEN</u>: What would <u>you</u> have done and said if you had been Job's wife in this situation?

<u>MEN</u>: What would you have told the wife if you had been Job?

B2. Do you think trials that God permits or discipline that He imposes have any impact on your life?

B3. What is your typical response, relative to God, in times of trial or suffering?

B4. What should it be?

B5. Do you relate more to the attitude of Job or to his wife?

Achan
he stole from God

Occurrences of "Achan" in the Bible: 7

Themes: Covetousness; Self-Reliance; Devoted Things

Achan's name occurs five times in Chapter 7 and once in Chapter 22 as an example of someone who defied God and the resulting impact of his sin:

> Josh 22:20   *Did not Achan the son of Zerah break faith in the matter of the devoted things, and wrath fell upon all the congregation of Israel? And he did not perish alone for his iniquity.* ESV

The name Achan also appears in 1 Chron 2:7 where it says:

> *The son of Carmi: Achan, the troubler of Israel, who broke faith in the matter of the devoted thing;* ESV

Scripture

Josh 7:1   Israel Defeated at Ai
But the people of Israel broke faith in regard to the devoted things, for Achan the son of Carmi, son of Zabdi, son of Zerah, of the tribe of Judah, took some of the devoted things. And the anger of the Lord burned against the people of Israel.

Josh 7:18-26
And he brought near his household man by man, and Achan the son of Carmi, son of Zabdi, son of Zerah, of the tribe of Judah, was taken. 19 Then Joshua said to Achan, "My son, give glory to the Lord God of Israel and give praise to him. And tell me now what you

have done; do not hide it from me." 20 And Achan answered Joshua, "Truly I have sinned against the Lord God of Israel, and this is what I did: 21 when I saw among the spoil a beautiful cloak from Shinar, and 200 shekels of silver, and a bar of gold weighing 50 shekels, then I coveted them and took them. And see, they are hidden in the earth inside my tent, with the silver underneath."

22 So Joshua sent messengers, and they ran to the tent; and behold, it was hidden in his tent with the silver underneath. 23 And they took them out of the tent and brought them to Joshua and to all the people of Israel. And they laid them down before the Lord. 24 And Joshua and all Israel with him took Achan the son of Zerah, and the silver and the cloak and the bar of gold, and his sons and daughters and his oxen and donkeys and sheep and his tent and all that he had. And they brought them up to the Valley of Achor. 25 And Joshua said, "Why did you bring trouble on us? The Lord brings trouble on you today." And all Israel stoned him with stones. They burned them with fire and stoned them with stones. 26 And they raised over him a great heap of stones that remains to this day. Then the Lord turned from his burning anger. Therefore, to this day the name of that place is called the Valley of Achor. ESV

The Context

Jericho

Led by Joshua, the Israelites had just scored a big victory over Jericho. It was their first intrusion into the Promised Land. Israel had never fought a battle as a nation – they were not warring people. They didn't really have an army. They were farmers, craftsmen, and sheep herders carrying weapons. The people of Jericho prided themselves on their thick walls that were considered to be impenetrable. So God delivered the victory to Israel at Jericho. Remember, they marched around the walls, shouted, and blew trumpets and the walls came tumbling down. There's probably a song in there somewhere!

Prior to attacking Jericho, Israel had prayed, consecrated themselves, and then obeyed God's instructions. But after the victory they were proud, overconfident, and maybe feeling a bit superior to everyone. They seemed to forget who won the victory as well as the instructions about the spoils of victory:

> Joshua 6:17-*18   And the city and all that is within it shall be devoted to the Lord for destruction. Only Rahab the prostitute and all who are with her in her house shall live, because she hid the messengers whom we sent. 18 But you, keep yourselves from the things devoted to destruction, lest when you have devoted them you take any of the devoted things and make the camp of Israel a thing for destruction and bring trouble upon it. ESV*

Devoted Things

Being "set apart" meant that it belonged to the Lord. The people were not to participate in any of the spoils of the victory at Jericho. This was decreed by God. The war booty was to be set aside and dedicated to the Lord for His treasury. Israel, however, was disobedient regarding these things set apart for God. Achan took some of the devoted things and God was angry with the Israelites.

"Devoted things" or "things set apart for destruction" meant they were to be given to God – irrevocably given. This means they either went to the Lord's treasury or they were to be totally destroyed, as in the case of the Canaanites when Israel was to take the Promised Land. Something "devoted" to God was forbidden from use by the people. These things were for God and God alone to be used at His sole discretion.

Defeat at Ai

The next enemy was Ai, and instead of doing all the things they did at Jericho to prepare for battle, the Israelites relied on themselves. They approached the battle with Ai much differently. They acted as if they were now great warriors and didn't really need God's help. They went from sheep herders to mighty soldiers overnight. They had experienced one single victory, in which they actually did nothing, and they thought they were an unbeatable war machine, so why ask God for help?

Joshua sent only some of the people out to face Ai. Joshua's spies advised him to send only a couple thousand troops. The spies' advice was that there would be no need to tire out all the people in what was likely to be another easy victory since only a few men were at Ai. But the result was much different than expected:

> Josh 7:5   *and the men of Ai killed about thirty-six of their men and chased them before the gate as far as Shebarim and struck them at the descent. And the hearts of the people melted and became as water.* ESV

Oops! Maybe the mighty warriors got a little ahead of themselves. If only 36 out of 3000 were struck down I would guess the rout was underway early in the battle – I assume Joshua's war machine switched to their running shoes and took flight early. Egos were damaged and Joshua began praying, lamenting, and frankly whining to God. He told God that He would lose face if He let the Canaanites wipe them out.

God told them that they had a traitor in their midst. Someone had violated the covenant about the things that were to be set apart and dedicated to God in the victory at Jericho. God said to Joshua:

> Josh 7:11-12   *Israel has sinned; they have transgressed my covenant . . . they have stolen and lied and put them among their own belongings. 12 Therefore the people of Israel cannot stand before their enemies. They turn their backs before their enemies, . . . I will be with you no more, unless you destroy the devoted things from among you.* ESV

What Do We Know?

Achan was the guilty party and he was found out! We don't know exactly how Achan was identified but God pointed at Him. It might have been by casting lots or some other selection method, but God led Joshua to Achan and he quickly confessed. He admitted that he had sinned against the Lord and told Joshua where the loot was hidden. One might wonder why Achan was so quick to confess since we know ahead of time what the sentence would be:

> Josh 7:15   *And he who is taken with the devoted things shall be burned with fire, he and all that he has, because he has transgressed the covenant of the Lord, and because he has done an outrageous thing in Israel.* ESV

Achan's lust was revealed and the text says he coveted the loot. He saw it. He wanted it. He coveted it. He took it. Then he hid it. Joshua retrieved the dedicated things from Achan's tent and spread them out for all to see.

The sentence was imposed! Achan was stoned and burned to death along with his family and the stolen loot! Achan, his family, and the devoted things were all buried under a heap of rocks and the Scripture tells us that the Lord then turned from His fierce anger against Israel.

Implications and Observations

Don't ignore God

If Joshua and the people had come to God first, as they had before Jericho, the Ai defeat would never have happened. God would have warned them in advance and they could have gotten right with Him before they went into battle. But they were overconfident and trusted in themselves, rather than relying on God to win the battle. When you think you are going to do it on your own and when your pride takes over, you're skating on thin ice.

You can't hide from God

Joshua was devastated by the defeat. Obviously God knows the things we try to hide from Him. Yet we act as if we can do things that God does not see. Maybe it's that we think He will just overlook our sin, or that disobedience is not a big deal to God. Looking around we can see all kinds of people who are disobeying God and who do not seem to be suffering repercussions in any way. But in this situation God dealt with Achan's sin very decisively and publically!

Achan did not make excuses, blame someone else, or suggest that the real cause was his environment as a child. When confronted he truthfully and completely admitted his guilt.

Be faithful with the little things

Problems often start with little things, like stealing a few trinkets, but they lead to bigger problems – in this case the death of 36 people in battle plus Achan and his whole family. Achan's sin led to a confrontation with God. The fleshly desires for things that look nice, smell nice, feel nice and taste nice can lead to serious consequences, particularly if they involve rebellion against God's instructions. Romans 13:14 gives us some advice: "*But put on the Lord Jesus Christ, and make no plans to satisfy the fleshly desires.*"

Discussion Questions

GENERAL

A1. Why do you think the sentence imposed on the guilty party was so great?

A2. What significance, if any, do you place on the fact that Achan knew exactly how many coins he stole and the exact weight of the gold?

A3. Why do you think that Joshua and the people were so confident of victory at Ai?

Q. Have you ever become overconfident? Have you ever thought you could do it all yourself and you really couldn't?

A4a. Do you think that Achan made himself right with God when he confessed and admitted what he did?

A4b. Since he confessed his sin, why was he punished?

A5. Why do you think Achan so openly and completely admitted his guilt? Why didn't he lie and hope to escape?

A6. What do you think people today would do if caught in the same circumstances?

A7. Why was the retribution against Achan effective?

A8. There is or should be a little real fear in "the fear of the Lord." Do you think people are afraid of God today?

Q. What are examples today where man seems to show no fear of God?

A9. What significance do you associate with the fact the "pile of rocks" remained visible long after the event?

A10. This story is about the disloyalty of one man, yet it impacted his whole family as well as the entire nation of Israel. How can you explain the magnitude of this impact, given he stole only a few trinkets and some money?

B. DIGGING DEEPER

B1. Was the sentence imposed on Achan, his family, and his animals fair? Should it be fair?

B2. Is God fair? Should God be fair?

Q. If you were given the choice of being treated with fairness, justice, or grace, which would you choose? Why?

B3. Can you find any other instances in Scripture where God's "burning anger"(7:1) is displayed? What does it mean that His anger burned against Israel?

B4. What does the passage say is the reason Achan stole the "things?" What does it mean?

B5. The advice of the spies in this case was not good. Can you think of another similar situation involving Joshua and spies?

B6. What's the moral of the story? If you were to pick one or two of the following, which are the best teachable lessons?

> a. Don't lose focus. Keep the main thing the main thing.
> b. Don't become self-absorbed, overconfident, and self-reliant.
> c. Nothing is too small or unimportant for God.
> d. How <u>quickly</u> we can revert from reliance on God to total self-reliance.
> e. You can't hide from God.
> f. What we do impacts those around us. There are consequences to our actions, and others often suffer those consequences.
> g. God knows everything.
> h. Don't place yourself on the wrong side of God!
> i. Don't be greedy.

C. JOSHUA'S PRAYER:

Josh 7:6-9 *Then Joshua tore his clothes and fell to the earth on his face before the ark of the Lord until the evening, he and the elders of Israel. And they put dust on their heads. 7 And Joshua said, "Alas, O Lord God, why have you brought this people over the Jordan at all, to give us into the hands of the Amorites, to destroy us? Would that we had been content to dwell beyond the Jordan! 8 O Lord, what can I say, when Israel has turned their backs before their enemies! 9 For the Canaanites and all the inhabitants of the land will hear of it and will surround us and cut off our name from the earth. And what will you do for your great name?"* ESV

C1. Specifically what did Joshua ask for in his prayer in 7:6-9? How would you describe this prayer?

C2. The portion of Joshua's prayer in 7:9 makes some sense in a twisted kind of way. If the Canaanites perceived that the invading Israelites were really all bluster and no substance, and that their God was not invincible, then that would reflect badly on God. The argument is this: "The enemy might actually stand up and fight and then what chance do we have against warriors? The resulting loss will reflect badly on You, God!" Do you buy this argument?

C3. How would you have prayed?

D. APPLICATION

D1. Do you have any sin in your life that needs to be dealt with? Do you think you are hiding anything from God?

D2. Have you ever taken God for granted? What happened?

D3. Are you underestimating the enemy?

F. THOUGHT QUESTION

We see in this situation that Israel was held corporately responsible for the ban on taking the things that were devoted to the Lord. Joshua 7:1, 11-12 makes it clear that all of Israel had sinned when one of their number defied God. So do you think that all of the people in the American church or all of the American people will be held accountable for the slavery, racial discrimination, abortion, same sex marriage, and the teaching of evolution in America?

Bezalel (Bezaleel)
the gifted craftsman

Occurrences of "Bezalel" in the Bible: 12

Themes: Spiritual Gifts; Skills; Worship

Scripture

Ex 31:1-11 Oholiab and Bezalel

The Lord said to Moses, 2 "See, I have called by name Bezalel the son of Uri, son of Hur, of the tribe of Judah, 3 and I have filled him with the Spirit of God, with ability and intelligence, with knowledge and all craftsmanship, 4 to devise artistic designs, to work in gold, silver, and bronze, 5 in cutting stones for setting, and in carving wood, to work in every craft. 6 And behold, I have appointed with him Oholiab, the son of Ahisamach, of the tribe of Dan. And I have given to all able men ability, that they may make all that I have commanded you: 7 the tent of meeting, and the ark of the testimony, and the mercy seat that is on it, and all the furnishings of the tent, 8 the table and its utensils, and the pure lampstand with all its utensils, and the altar of incense, 9 and the altar of burnt offering with all its utensils, and the basin and its stand, 10 and the finely worked garments, the holy garments for Aaron the priest and the garments of his sons, for their service as priests, 11 and the anointing oil and the fragrant incense for the Holy Place. According to all that I have commanded you, they shall do."

Ex 35:34   *And he has inspired him to teach, both him and Oholiab the son of Ahisamach of the tribe of Dan.*

Ex 36:1-4   *"Bezalel and Oholiab and every craftsman in whom the Lord has put skill and intelligence to know how to do any work in the construction of the sanctuary shall work in accordance with all that the Lord has commanded." 2 And Moses called Bezalel and Oholiab and every craftsman in whose mind the Lord had put skill, everyone whose heart stirred him up to come to do the work. 3 And they received from Moses all the contribution that the people of Israel had brought for doing the work on the sanctuary. They still kept bringing him freewill offerings every morning,* ESV

NOTE: Chapters 35-39 in Exodus list and tell all of the items and furnishing that Bezalel and his workers made. The remaining uses of Bezalel's name are listings in genealogies, or repeating facts already in the Scripture above.

The Context

Israel had been led out of Egypt and across the Red Sea to Mt. Sinai where they were given the Ten Commandments. After a brief hiccup with a Golden Calf, Moses went up the mountain again where he received a second set of Commandments and instructions for worship. The people were to construct a tabernacle for worship and to serve as the place where God would reside in their presence.

In the preceding chapters God had told Moses about all the things he and the people would need to make: priestly garments, furniture, furnishings, equipment, altars, and the tabernacle itself. There was a great amount of work to do to build and prepare the tabernacle for worship. In addition the people were asked to give offerings of money, gems, linen, yarn, gold, silver, skins, wood, and almost anything and everything that would provide the necessary material to build and construct all the items for the tabernacle, or Tent of Meeting. The Israelites brought freewill offerings to the Lord for everything that had been commanded of them (35:29).

The people were so generous that Moses finally had to tell them to stop bringing offerings (36:6-7).

What Do We Know?

The text indicates that both Bezalel and Oholiab were filled with the Holy Spirit, with skill, ability, and knowledge in all kinds of crafts to do all the required work. In addition, they were both given the ability by God to teach others to do the work. God also gave others the skill and know how to carry out the work. God chose Bezalel, put him in charge, and then raised up people capable of doing both the skilled work and common work necessary to construct the tabernacle.

Bezalel and his band of workers would have been extremely busy. Oholiab was appointed to help Bezalel (31:6), and chapters 37-39 provide an outline of all the things that Bezalel and his workers made: the tabernacle, the Ark, the table, the lampstand, the altars, the basin, the courtyard, the priestly garments, the ephod, the breastpiece, the robe, and all the other required utensils and furnishings. When they were finished, they brought everything to Moses for inspection:

> Exodus 39:42-43   *The Israelites had done all the work according to everything the Lord had commanded Moses. 43 Moses inspected all the work they had accomplished. They had done just as the Lord commanded. Then Moses blessed them.*

Moses did not recruit or appoint any of the workers. Scripture states that God specifically appointed Bezalel by name. And since God will equip those He calls into service, Bezalel and all the others received God-given skills to do the work required to build and furnish the tabernacle. The same skill and knowledge was _not_ given to Moses. God delegated the work to Bezalel and his workers. But Moses had the final review as everything that was made was brought to him for approval. Bezalel did not have the authority to approve the work, only to do the work.

There were no rewards or punishments mentioned for doing or not doing the work. It appears there were people to do all the work.

Moses put out a call and the faithful showed up. Nothing is said about doing shoddy work or anyone grumbling about the hours, the nature of the work, or the fact they were not getting paid to do this work.

Implications and Observations

Scripture doesn't tell us if Bezalel and the workers who were given skill and knowledge already had some of the skills they needed to do their assigned tasks. But given that they had been slaves in Egypt, it is unlikely that they had much (if any) skill in fine workmanship. Bezalel in particular was given knowledge and skill in a large number of different specialized areas. It seems reasonable to conclude that the workers were given new skills by God in order to do the kind and quality of work He required.

When Moses called for those with skill and abilities to come forward to do the work, they came willingly. There is no report of lack of workers or lack of skill. There is no report of Bezalel coming to Moses requesting more help.

The workers were given a "heart" for the work they would be doing:

> Exodus 36:2   *So Moses summoned Bezalel, Oholiab, and every skilled person in whose heart the Lord had placed wisdom, everyone whose heart moved him, to come to the work and do it*

When God wants work done He not only provides the skill and ability to do the work, but also a heart for the work. The people desired to be involved in this work and they came forward willingly when Moses put out a call for workers. Even though the Israelites were notorious for their grumbling, we see no evidence in these chapters that the people were unhappy or unwilling to do the work. This would have been exciting and satisfying work – constructing a place for worship and making all the things needed for the tabernacle. Remember, the people had never had a place like this or the potential of God to "be with them."

Everything the craftsmen were doing was new. The people had not worshipped in this manner before, so there were probably many questions about the use and purpose of the items they were constructing. There would have been curiosity, awe, wonder, excitement, and confusion all at the same time. There were no traditions yet established. The whole idea of a Sabbath and the requirement for offerings and sacrifices would have been major topics of discussion, both while they worked, and around their campfires at night. The mood in the camp was likely one of excitement, anticipation, and maybe some fear and trepidation.

Why fear? The people were not very far removed from being slaves in Egypt. Living on their own, needing to survive in the wilderness, and now a whole new set of rules to satisfy their God would have put an edge to all they were doing. How long would God feed them? What would they do when their clothes wore out and their sandals fell off their feet? How would they find enough water to survive? Did Moses really know what he was doing? Could Bezalel make all these new things so that God would be satisfied? What would happen if God rejected the work of the craftsmen? What other rules might God impose on their lives? Would they ever get to live in the Promised Land?

Discussion Questions

GENERAL

A1. Find in your study Bible, Bible dictionary, or commentary the meaning of the names Bezalel and Oholiab. How do they fit with how God used Bezalel?

A2. How would you assess the importance of the work that was assigned to Bezalel and his craftsmen?

Q. Do you think there were people urging them to hurry?

Q. Do you think there were people secretly wanting a long delay?

Q. Could the people have been fearful of God's presence?

A3. Do you think it would make any difference if Bezalel didn't make the items to the exact requirements? Why? What might have been the result if Bezalel had not made everything exactly as specified?

Q. How would you have felt if Moses rejected your work?

A4. Why did Moses have the final approval on everything that was made by Bezalel and his men?

A5. Do you think that Bezalel understood the general nature and purpose of what they were doing?

A6. Let's assume some of the items were "more important" than others because they had "spiritual significance." Do you think it would have been appropriate to distinguish between these items and assign them to the most gifted craftsmen?

A7. Do you think most of the people knew what was going on with the construction? [If there were 200 people working and the number of people in the camp was 2,000,000 = $1/100^{th}$ of 1 percent]

A8. How would you imagine the people working on the project felt about each other? Why?

A9. The tabernacle was something new, and the items the craftsmen were making had never been seen or used before. Can you imagine for a moment the conversation they would have had as they made all the required furnishings and utensils? What do you suppose they were asking each other? Choose one item listed below from Chapters 37-39 and list several questions that the workmen may have asked each other about that item.

ITEMS: Ark – table – lampstand – altar of incense – altar of burnt offering – bronze basin – courtyard – ephod – breastpiece – robe – tunics – turban – headbands – undergarments – holy diadem – medallion – tent.

A10. How important was the skill to teach others? Why do you think this particular skill was given to the leaders? Do you think it would have been better to have fewer people involved in the construction and allowed the highly skilled people gifted by God do most of the work? Why? Why not?

A11. How does this story fit with or contrast to the answer to the question, "What is the chief purpose or end of man?"

A12. In Ex 36:2 the text indicates the people had a heart to do the work. Do you think this occurs with all spiritual gifts? Do we all have a "heart" for doing the work of our spiritual gifts? What are the implications?

B. WHAT's GOING ON?

B1. Bezalel was constructing a tabernacle (Tent of the Meeting) and was making furnishings and utensils to be used in the tabernacle. Sacrifices and offerings would be brought to the tabernacle, but it was more! What else did all this represent? [Hint: see 25:8b]

Q. What do you suppose the people thought it meant that God was going to dwell among them?

B2. What was the unique significance of Exodus 37:5?
Exodus 37:5   *He inserted the poles into the rings on the sides of the ark for carrying the ark.*

During the conquest of Canaan by the Israelites, the tabernacle remained at Gilgal, while the Ark of the Covenant was evidently carried from place to place with the armies of Israel. The Ark was reported at the crossing of the Jordan (Josh 3:6), at Gilgal (Josh 4:11), at the conquest of Jericho (Josh 6:4), at the campaigns against Ai (Josh 7:6), and at Mount Ebal (Josh 8:33). [1 (Nelson's)]

B3. What do you think is the most important information, lesson, or observation for the church today in this story? Why?

B4. Why do you think God gave such specific and detailed instructions? Why didn't He just tell them to make a box, or basin, or altar, etc.?

B5. Bezalel and his workman constructed a tabernacle. There was only one. There was only ever one temple. Why do Christians <u>not</u> have a central place to worship? Many other religions have a special holy place.

C. SUBJECT – Time

C1. What were all the other people and Moses doing during this time of construction?

Q. If someone were praying, what might they have been praying about?

C2. How do you think the people who were not participating in the work felt about the work?

D. APPLICATION

D1. Has God gifted you with any *skill* to use in His service? Do you have a skill you could teach another believer?

D2. Are you using your *spiritual gifts* in doing the work God has called you to?

D3. Do you have a heart for something? Are you using that interest or skill for the work of God?

D4. How will you respond to God if He says, "I gave you these skills and gifts to use for these opportunities? What did you do with them?" How would you respond?

D5. What in this lesson do you personally want to remember?

Jeduthun
a worship leader

Occurrences of "Jeduthun" in the Bible: 14

Themes: Praise; Worship

Scripture

<u>1 Chron 16:39-42</u>
And he left Zadok the priest and his brothers the priests before the tabernacle of the Lord in the high place that was at Gibeon 40 to offer burnt offerings to the Lord on the altar of burnt offering regularly morning and evening, to do all that is written in the Law of the Lord that he commanded Israel. 41 With them were Heman and Jeduthun and the rest of those chosen and expressly named to give thanks to the Lord, for his steadfast love endures forever. 42 Heman and Jeduthun had trumpets and cymbals for the music and instruments for sacred song. The sons of Jeduthun were appointed to the gate. ESV

<u>1 Chron 25:1-6</u>
David and the chiefs of the service also set apart for the service the sons of Asaph, and of Heman, and of Jeduthun, who prophesied with lyres, with harps, and with cymbals. The list of those who did the work and of their duties was: 2 Of the sons of Asaph: Zaccur, Joseph, Nethaniah, and Asharelah, sons of Asaph, under the direction of Asaph, who prophesied under the direction of the king. 3 Of Jeduthun, the sons of Jeduthun: Gedaliah, Zeri, Jeshaiah,

Shimei, Hashabiah, and Mattithiah, six, under the direction of their father Jeduthun, who prophesied with the lyre in thanksgiving and praise to the Lord. 4 Of Heman, the sons of Heman: Bukkiah, Mattaniah, Uzziel, Shebuel and Jerimoth, Hananiah, Hanani, Eliathah, Giddalti, and Romamti-ezer, Joshbekashah, Mallothi, Hothir, Mahazioth. 5 All these were the sons of Heman the king's seer, according to the promise of God to exalt him, for God had given Heman fourteen sons and three daughters. 6 They were all under the direction of their father in the music in the house of the Lord with cymbals, harps, and lyres for the service of the house of God. Asaph, Jeduthun, and Heman were under the order of the king. ESV

2 Chron 5:12
and all the Levitical singers, Asaph, Heman, and Jeduthun, their sons and kinsmen, arrayed in fine linen, with cymbals, harps, and lyres, stood east of the altar with 120 priests who were trumpeters; ESV

2 Chron 35:15
The singers, the sons of Asaph, were in their place according to the command of David, and Asaph, and Heman, and Jeduthun the king's seer; and the gatekeepers were at each gate. They did not need to depart from their service, for their brothers the Levites prepared for them. ESV

The Context

Jeduthun
Jeduthun was chosen and appointed by king David to give thanks unto the Lord "for His mercy endures forever" (1 Chronicles 16:41:42). His service was distinct as he was appointed to prophesy with lyres, harps and cymbals, giving thanks and praising the Lord (1 Chronicles 25:1, 3). Interestingly, the meaning of the name Jeduthun in Hebrew is "praising." Jeduthun is also referred to as the king's seer (2 Chronicles 35:15).

<u>David</u>

In Chapter 11 of 1 Chronicles David became king of Israel. Saul had died at the hands of the Lord and He turned over the kingdom to David. After David consolidated his position as king one of the first things he wanted to do was bring the Ark of the Covenant back to the people and the nation agreed. But there were problems in transportation, and the Ark was initially taken to the house of Obed-Edom where it remained for three months.

David prepared a place for the Ark in Jerusalem and he called on the Levites to consecrate themselves in order to bring the Ark into the City of David properly. The Ark had not been transported in the prescribed way on the first attempt but now with the Levites in command of the travel arrangements, all went well and the Ark was brought to the tent that David had prepared. On that day David wrote a psalm of thanksgiving (1 Chron 16:8-36) to celebrate the return of the Ark. It was a call to worship their God.

Upon the reading or singing of this psalm the people said "Amen" and "Praise the Lord."

What Do We Know?

Jeduthun and his six sons were part of the worship team that David initially appointed to be responsible for continuing worship at the tabernacle in Gibeon. The priests were appointed to offer burnt sacrifices daily and to do all that the law commanded. Heman was appointed along with Jeduthun, and they had trumpets, cymbals, and other instruments for presenting sacred songs.

Approximately thirty years later Jeduthun and his family were one of the three family groups responsible for leading the 4000 Levitical musicians leading worship (1 Chron 25:1-6). Jeduthun's leadership and talent was evident in that his name appears at the top of Psalms 39, 62, and 77, probably indicating that his choir was to sing the psalm.

Jeduthun's family is again mentioned at the dedication of Solomon's temple wherein the descendants of the three chief choir masters (Asaph, Heman, and Jeduthun) were said to be dressed in fine linen and participating with the priests at the dedication of the temple (2Chron 5:12).

Discussion Questions

A. DAVID BECOMES KING

A1. What musical instruments are listed as being used in worship?

1 Chron 16:42: _____.
1 Chron 25:1: _____.
1 Chron 25:3: _____.
1 Chron 25:6: _____.
2 Chron 5:12: _____.

A2. What did the priests do daily at Gibeon (1 Chron 16:40)?

A3. What were Heman and Jeduthun to do?

Q. How is this consistent with David's Psalm of Thanks (see 1 Chron 16:23-25).

A4. Do you think there is a difference between the trumpets and cymbals to be used for music and the instruments to be used for sacred songs?

A5. What is the significance of the fact that those leading the worship were "expressly named"?

B. DAVID ORGANIZED WORSHIP

B1. Is it Jeduthun who was set apart to serve (25:1)?

B2. It does not say that the sons sang or played instruments. What does it say and what does it mean?

B3. How might the description of the musicians prophesying through their instruments be similar to the functions of a prophet?

B4. We observe that Heman was described as the king's seer. In 2 Chron 35:15 Jeduthun is also described as the king's seer. What do you think that means?

B5. What interesting or surprising fact do we learn in 25:5-6?

Q. Why might this be surprising?

C. WORSHIP

C1. Define "worship" in your own words. Write out several sentences or make a list of characteristics of worship.

C2. A "burnt offering" is described in Leviticus 1 and is defined as a voluntary offering by fire that is a soothing aroma to the Lord. When the person making the sacrifice lays his hand on the head of the burnt offering (sacrifice), what was to have happened?

Q. What does atonement mean?

C3. What was the purpose of the tabernacle and ultimately the temple?

C4. The first thing a worshipper encountered after entering the tabernacle was the bronze altar. The first nine chapters of Leviticus describe seven different offerings to be brought to the bronze altar. Here we are interested only in the burnt offering.
Leviticus 1:3-5   If his offering is a burnt offering from the herd, he shall offer a male without blemish. He shall bring it to the entrance of the tent of meeting, that he may be accepted before the Lord. 4 He shall lay his hand on the head of the burnt offering, and it shall be accepted for him to make atonement for him. 5 Then he shall kill the bull before the Lord, and Aaron's sons the priests shall bring the blood and throw the blood against the sides of the altar that is at the entrance of the tent of meeting. ESV

Q. Why would a worshipper lay his hand on the head of the animal?

Q. Who killed the animal and why?

C5. The bronze altar was the first piece of furniture or station in the tabernacle. What does that tell us about approaching God to worship Him?

C6. What did the Ark of the Covenant represent?

C7. What did the mercy seat represent?

C8. The Ark of the Covenant represented the throne or the presence of God. There was a curtain (veil) in the tabernacle that separated the room that contained the Ark (the Holy of Holies) from the room called the Holy Place that contained the golden lampstand, showbread, and the altar of incense. No one entered the Holy of Holies except once per year on the Day of Atonement (Lev 16:2). On the day of Jesus' crucifixion the veil was torn in two from top to bottom (Matt 27:51).

Q. What did the tearing of the veil from top to bottom mean?

D. APPLICATION

Because of the completed work of Christ, we are cleansed once and for all and we are able to enter into the very throne room of God, through His only begotten Son who shed His life's blood so that our sins were covered. Our response then should be that we worship Him, presenting our lives as a living sacrifice, which is now holy and acceptable to God! (Rom 12:1)

D1. Do you have a problem in that those participating in worship had to qualify and be chosen or do you think anyone should be allowed to be on a worship team?

D2. How would you feel about working (church or secular) under the direction of your father?

D3. Do you ever feel God's presence in the lyrics or melody of the worship music? If so, when does that usually happen?

Q. Have you ever felt you received a message from God through the worship music?

D4. Do you think your worship is authentic? Why? Why not?

D5. Do you truly understand and appreciate that Jesus had to die (shed His blood) for you personally? How do you react to that understanding?

The Watchman
a lookout on the wall

Occurrences of "watchman" in the Bible: 28

Themes: Prophets; Rebuke

Scripture

The Prophet was the designated watchman:

Ezek 3:17   *Son of man, I have made you a watchman for the house of Israel. Whenever you hear a word from my mouth, you shall give them warning from me.* ESV

Isa 62:6-7   *On your walls, O Jerusalem, I have set watchmen; all the day and all the night they shall never be silent. You who put the Lord in remembrance, take no rest, 7 and give him no rest until he establishes Jerusalem and makes it a praise in the earth.* ESV

Condemnation of the people:

Jer 6:17   *I set watchmen over you, saying, 'Pay attention to the sound of the trumpet!' But they said, 'We will not pay attention.'*

Ezekiel - Israel's last watchman

Ezek 33:2-8   *"Son of man, speak to your people and say to them, If I bring the sword upon a land, and the people of the land take a man from among them, and make him their watchman, 3 and if he sees the sword coming upon the land and blows the trumpet and warns the people, 4 then if anyone who hears the sound of the trumpet does not take warning, and the sword comes and takes him away, his blood shall be upon his own head. 5 He heard the sound of the trumpet and did not take warning; his blood shall be upon himself. But if he had taken warning, he would have saved his life. 6 But if the watchman sees the sword coming and does not blow the trumpet, so that the people are not warned, and the sword comes and takes any one of them, that person is taken away in his iniquity, but his blood I will require at the watchman's hand. 7 "So you, son of man, I have made a watchman for the house of Israel. Whenever you hear a word from my mouth, you shall give them warning from me."* ESV.

The Context

In ancient times every city and town of any size had watchmen. They were posted on the walls surrounding the city or in watchtowers. Their job was to warn the city of invaders or any other approaching dangers. The watchman was a sentinel – one who was to be vigilant and alert to any possible danger or problem.

The prophet's role as a watchman was to warn God's people, including their leaders, to repent from their wicked ways. Just as a tower watchman was to warn the people of coming dangers, so the prophet's responsibility was to warn Israel about their sin and the coming danger of God's righteous judgment if they did not obey His commands.

What Do We Know?

Isaiah, Jeremiah, and Ezekiel (all major prophets) were appointed as watchmen by God. Their primary purpose as watchmen was to warn the people and the nation about their sinful actions and call them to repentance:

> Ezekiel 18:30-32   *"Therefore I will judge you, O house of Israel, every one according to his ways, declares the Lord God. Repent and turn from all your transgressions, lest iniquity be your ruin. 31 Cast away from you all the transgressions that you have committed, and make*

yourselves a new heart and a new spirit! Why will you die, O house of Israel? 32 For I have no pleasure in the death of anyone, declares the Lord God; so turn, and live." ESV

The prophet watchmen carried out their responsibilities but the people and their leaders did not respond. Jeremiah 16:7 says they did not even listen!

Israel's Leaders – Shepherds

God appointed the prophet watchmen to warn both the people and the leaders. The leaders were to be the shepherds of Israel, watching over their flock day and night, just as the watchmen were to be vigilant both day and night (Isaiah 62:6-7). Prophets and watchmen were appointed to warn Israel because their leaders were not doing the job of a shepherd: leading, watching, protecting, defending, and caring for the people.

If the shepherd leaders had been doing their jobs, watchmen would not have been necessary. But the kings and religious leaders, who should have acted as watchmen, failed in their responsibility to lead by example. The leaders were no better than the people. Shepherd leaders should have been protecting the people from the predators around them, but instead they led the people into idolatry and rebellion. Isaiah describes the situation as follows:

> Isaiah 56:9-12   *All you beasts of the field, come to devour—all you beasts in the forest. 10 His watchmen are blind; they are all without knowledge; they are all silent dogs; they cannot bark, dreaming, lying down, loving to slumber. 11 The dogs have a mighty appetite; they never have enough. But they are shepherds who have no understanding; they have all turned to their own way, each to his own gain, one and all. 12 "Come," they say, "let me get wine; let us fill ourselves with strong drink; and tomorrow will be like this day, great beyond measure."* ESV

The leaders, instead of looking out for the people, had become self-indulgent and self-righteous. Verse 12 above is a sad commentary on the condition of the shepherd leaders. So the word from the prophet watchmen was as much for the leaders as it was for the people.

Discussion Questions

GENERAL

A1. Who were these prophet watchmen and what was their primary job?

A2. Describe the normal watchman (not the prophet watchman).

A3. The prophet watchmen generally called the people and the nation to repentance. Why did the people need to repent?

Generally:

Specifically:

A4. What does it mean to admonish or rebuke someone?

Admonish:

Rebuke:

A5. Do you think that "warning" includes or should include rebuke?

A6. How would you describe the life of a watchman (based on Isa 62:6-7)?

Q. Do you know anyone who is totally immersed in their work or ministry such that they could be described as getting no rest?

A7. What do you learn about watchman in each one of the passages below?

> Micah 7:4   *The best of them is like a brier, the most upright of them a thorn hedge. The day of your watchmen, of your punishment, has come; now their confusion is at hand.* ESV

> Isaiah 62:1   *For Zion's sake I will not keep silent, and for Jerusalem's sake I will not be quiet, until her righteousness goes forth as brightness, and her salvation as a burning torch.* ESV

> Isaiah 56:10   *His watchmen are blind; they are all without knowledge; they are all silent dogs; they cannot bark, dreaming, lying down, loving to slumber.* ESV

A8. Review Ezekiel 33:2-7 above. Who is held accountable?

Q. Does this mean the people are not held responsible for their disobedience?

A9. Do you think Ezekiel 33:2-7 is "fair"? How would you explain?

Q. If your answer is no, what then would be fair?

Q. If your answer above is yes, what then would not be fair?

A10. How would you evaluate the job of the watchman prophets? Did they do their job? How well did they do?

A11. What was the purpose of the watchman prophets? God appointed these men and most of the prophet watchmen did a reasonable job. They warned the people and called Israel to repent, but their words fell on deaf ears. So, what was their purpose? God knew in advance that the people were not going to respond. He even told the prophets that their words would be ignored and destruction was a sure result of their behavior. So why did God bother?

A12. What characteristic of the Jewish people (and us as well) made the leadership of Israel so important? [See Jeremiah 50:6]

A13. What does Hosea 9:8 mean for the watchman?
Hosea 9:8   *The prophet is the watchman of Ephraim with my God; yet a fowler's snare is on all his ways, and hatred in the house of his God.* ESV

B. TODAY

B1. Do you know any watchmen in the church today?

      a) Who are they?
      b) What are they saying?
      c) Do they have a following?

B2. Do you think America needs watchmen today at the national level? Why? Why not?

B3. How would you describe today's watchmen compared to watchmen described in the Old Testament?

B4. If you were personally appointed as a watchman for America, what would you do or say? Write a press release of 20-40 words to be sent out on social media on what you want the church to know today.

B5. Do you think each of us should be held responsible as watchmen? Can you think of any New Testament passage that would support or reject this concept?

C. APPLICATION

C1. Would you be willing to be a watchman? Why? Why not?

C2. If God were to ask you to be a watchman, what would He want you to watch over? Who would God think you could influence or take responsibility for?

C3. As a watchman what do you perceive is the first thing God would ask you to do?

Shear-Jashub
son of Isaiah

Occurrences of "Shear-Jashub" in the Bible: 1

Themes: the Remnant

Scripture

Isa 6:11-13   Isaiah's Calling
Then I said, "How long, O Lord?" And he said: "Until cities lie waste without inhabitant, and houses without people, and the land is a desolate waste, 12 and the Lord removes people far away, and the forsaken places are many in the midst of the land. 13 And though a tenth remain in it, it will be burned again, like a terebinth or an oak, whose stump remains when it is felled." The holy seed is its stump.

Isa 7:1-6   Isaiah Sent to King Ahaz
In the days of Ahaz the son of Jotham, son of Uzziah, king of Judah, Rezin the king of Syria and Pekah the son of Remaliah the king of Israel came up to Jerusalem to wage war against it, but could not yet mount an attack against it. 2 When the house of David was told, "Syria is in league with Ephraim," the heart of Ahaz and the heart of his people shook as the trees of the forest shake before the wind. 3 And the Lord said to Isaiah, "Go out to meet Ahaz, you and Shear-jashub your son, at the end of the conduit of the upper pool on the highway to the Washer's Field. 4 And say to him, 'Be careful,

be quiet, do not fear, and do not let your heart be faint because of these two smoldering stumps of firebrands, at the fierce anger of Rezin and Syria and the son of Remaliah. 5 Because Syria, with Ephraim and the son of Remaliah, has devised evil against you, saying, 6 "Let us go up against Judah and terrify it, and let us conquer it for ourselves, and set up the son of Tabeel as king in the midst of it,"

Isa 10:20-23   The Remnant of Israel Will Return

20 In that day the remnant of Israel and the survivors of the house of Jacob will no more lean on him who struck them, but will lean on the Lord, the Holy One of Israel, in truth. 21 A remnant will return, the remnant of Jacob, to the mighty God. 22 For though your people Israel be as the sand of the sea, only a remnant of them will return. Destruction is decreed, overflowing with righteousness. 23 For the Lord God of hosts will make a full end, as decreed, in the midst of all the earth.

Isa 37:4, 30-35   God Promises and Delivers

It may be that the Lord your God will hear the words of the Rabshakeh, whom his master the king of Assyria has sent to mock the living God, and will rebuke the words that the Lord your God has heard; therefore lift up your prayer for the remnant that is left.'". . . 30 "And this shall be the sign for you: this year you shall eat what grows of itself, and in the second year what springs from that. Then in the third year sow and reap, and plant vineyards, and eat their fruit. 31 And the surviving remnant of the house of Judah shall again take root downward and bear fruit upward. 32 For out of Jerusalem shall go a remnant, and out of Mount Zion a band of survivors. The zeal of the Lord of hosts will do this. 33 "Therefore thus says the Lord concerning the king of Assyria: He shall not come into this city or shoot an arrow there or come before it with a shield or cast up a siege mound against it. 34 By the way that he came, by the same he shall return, and he shall not come into this city, declares the Lord. 35 For I will defend this city to save it, for my own sake and for the sake of my servant David." ESV

The Context

Historical Setting

Isaiah was a prophet who was chosen by God in 740 BC, the year King Uzziah died. He spent most of his ministry in and around Jerusalem. He had two sons, Shear-Jashub, the focus of this study, and Maher-Shalal-Hash-Baz (8:3). Most of what Isaiah wrote about in the first 39 chapters occurred during his ministry. Because of this, many believe that the book was written about 701 BC, the year the Assyrian army was destroyed after they had conquered the Northern Kingdom in 722-21 BC. Thus, the writing occurred after the first exile but before the second exile of Judah (Southern Kingdom). Jerusalem was captured by the Babylonians in 586 BC.

It is not always clear if Isaiah is referring to one of the divided kingdoms or to the combined nation of Israel. When it's important to know the specific target of Isaiah's writing, a careful study is required. We are focusing on "the remnant" in this study, which applies to both kingdoms and to the total nation of Israel, so determining the particular target of Isaiah's prophecy is not usually required.

The Story

The first six chapters of Isaiah outline a series of promises and rebukes. Charges were leveled against Judah (the Southern Kingdom) for breaking the covenant, but the text indicates the nation would ultimately be restored – only after judgment. Chapters 3-5 contain oracles of both woe and hope. God's people were living in rebellion. They were living an illusion because of the absence of justice, righteousness, and faithfulness. Chapter 5 begins with the Song of the Vineyard, an indictment against Israel, and ends by proclaiming woes which would lead to Judah's judgment because of greed, pleasure, self-deception, rejection of God's word, and injustice. The result in 5:24 was fire, decay, and being blown away – because they spurned the word of the Holy One of Israel.

In chapter 6 we have the unique calling of Isaiah as a prophet, combined with the beginning of the theme about a King who reigns in Zion:

      a. 6:1, 5 the Lord (God, the Father).
      b. 7:1-2 the current King (Pekah [Israel]; Ahaz [Judah]).
      c. 9:6-7 a King yet to come (the Messiah).

The land had to be judged because of the sin of the people, but God was faithful. He would leave a "tenth" (the remnant) in the land (6:13).

In chapter seven we meet the son of Isaiah, Shear-Jashub, whose name means, "a remnant will return." He may have been Isaiah's oldest son and he had a symbolic name reminding us that God will always have a people. There will always be a faithful remnant that survives God's judgment.

What Do We Know?

In the first eleven chapters of Isaiah, even in the midst of indictments against Israel, the promise of a surviving remnant is very clear. For example:

> Isaiah 1:9   *If the Lord of hosts had not left us a few survivors, we should have been like Sodom, and become like Gomorrah.* ESV
> Isaiah 10:20   *In that day the remnant of Israel and the survivors of the house of Jacob will no more lean on him who struck them, but will lean on the Lord, the Holy One of Israel, in truth.* ESV

We see in 1:27 that Zion is restored. The promise of restoration is also described in chapter 2:

> Isaiah 1:27   *Zion shall be redeemed by justice, and those in her who repent, by righteousness.* ESV
> Isaiah 2:2-3   *It shall come to pass in the latter days that the mountain of the house of the Lord shall be established*

*as the highest of the mountains, and shall be lifted up
above the hills; and all the nations shall flow to it, 3 and
many peoples shall come, and say: "Come, let us go up to
the mountain of the Lord, to the house of the God of Jacob,
that he may teach us his ways and that we may walk in his
paths." For out of Zion shall go the law, and the word of the
Lord from Jerusalem.* ESV   [see also Isa 4:2-4]

In addition, Isaiah 8:11-22 describes a believing remnant, a people
of hope. That hope is assured by a royal child who will be called
Wonderful Counselor, Mighty God, Prince of Peace (9:1-7). Isaiah
the Prophet was called to warn Judah that her sins would lead to
exile at the hands of the Babylonians. But Isaiah's message also
included the promise that ultimately God would have mercy on His
people:

> Isaiah 14:1-2   Israel's Return
> *For the Lord will have compassion on Jacob and will again
> choose Israel, and will set them in their own land, and
> sojourners will join them and will attach themselves to the
> house of Jacob. 2 And the peoples will take them and bring
> them to their place, and the house of Israel will possess
> them in the Lord's land as male and female slaves. They will
> take captive those who were their captors, and rule over
> those who oppressed them.* ESV

The future of Israel was confirmed and assured, but the present
reality was that before that wonderful day in the future, a real and
devastating judgment would be exacted on the people of God
because of their injustice, unrighteousness, and unfaithfulness. But
God will always have a people – *the remnant*!

Implications and Observations

We do not know the circumstances that led to Isaiah naming his
son Shear-Jashub (*a remnant shall return*). Maybe the Lord spoke
to him and requested that name, but that seems unlikely because
that request would have been important enough to record in the
book of Isaiah. It is more likely that Isaiah had full confidence in the

Lord and wanted to send the dual message of sound and sight – his words and his son. In an age when the meaning of names was highly significant, choosing the name Shear-Jashub would have been a clear, visual, and living message to the people.

The calling and acceptance of Isaiah in Isa 6:5-9 might be described as a metaphor for Israel the nation or Judah the Kingdom:

> Isaiah 6:5-9   And I said: "Woe is me! For I am lost; for I am a man of unclean lips, and I dwell in the midst of a people of unclean lips; for my eyes have seen the King, the Lord of hosts!" 6 Then one of the seraphim flew to me, having in his hand a burning coal that he had taken with tongs from the altar. 7 And he touched my mouth and said: "Behold, this has touched your lips; your guilt is taken away, and your sin atoned for. Isaiah's Commission from the Lord 8 And I heard the voice of the Lord saying, "Whom shall I send, and who will go for us?" Then I said, "Here am I! Send me." 9 And he said, "Go, and say to this people: 'Keep on hearing, but do not understand; keep on seeing, but do not perceive.'" ESV

Here we see Isaiah's sinfulness and a description of the people as having unclean lips. Their sin was even greater and more obvious when compared to the Lord of Hosts (6:5). In order to cleanse Isaiah, a hot coal touched the prophet's lips. The purification (6:6) is a metaphor indicating the Prophet's lips would be the instrument God would use to declare the sin of the people. The cleansing agent was sent by God in the form of a seraphim and the burning coal came from the altar – the place where sacrifices were offered in atonement for sins (6:6-7). There is a significant contrast between Isaiah and the people. Isaiah immediately volunteered to serve the Lord (6:8), while the people ignored both the prophet and his message of repentance (6:9).

Discussion Questions

GENERAL

A. ISAIAH

A1. In 6:8 Isaiah makes a personal choice. What about Israel and the people of Israel?

    Q. What is the choice for Israel?

    Q. Is it a corporate or an individual choice?

A2. In 6:11 Isaiah asks how long he should preach. Or, how long is this going to take and what's going to happen? What is the answer?

a. Message of DOOM:

b. Message of HOPE:

B. SHEAR-JASHUB

B1. The name Shear-Jashub was intended to be both a warning and a word of hope to Israel. Explain.

a. WARNING:

b. HOPE:

B2. What does the symbolic naming of Isaiah's son tell you about what Isaiah believed?

B3. What does 8:18 tell us about what Isaiah and his son would become? What kind of sign would the son be to Israel?
Isaiah 8:18   *Behold, I and the children whom the Lord has given me are signs and portents in Israel from the Lord of hosts, who dwells on Mount Zion.* ESV

B4. If the people generally believed the concept of the remnant, what might they have believed about who was in the remnant?

Q. How would you draw a comparison with the remnant in Isaiah's time and the American church today?

B5. In Isa 10:21 we have the meaning of Shear-Jashub ("a remnant will return") applied to Jacob (Israel). That thought is continued into 10:22. What is the implied nature of the remnant?
Isaiah 10:22   *For though your people Israel be as the sand of the sea, only a remnant of them will return. Destruction is decreed, overflowing with righteousness.* ESV

Q. Why might the size of the remnant resonate with the people?

C. THE REMNANT

C1. With regard to the Bible, and particularly the Old Testament, who or what was the remnant?

C2. Prior to the Exodus was there ever a "remnant"?

Q. How would you contrast the Jewish remnant, in general, with the Flood remnant?

The Problem
Flood: Sin and evil in general was rampant.
Jewish: _____.

The People
Flood: Applied to world.
Jewish: _____.

The Impact
Flood: Flood destroyed all but Noah and his family.
Jewish: _____.

C3. Do you think God was working against Himself by telling the people on one hand they must change or be destroyed and then assuring them that He would save a remnant?

C4. If you had been living in those times, would you have understood the prophet's message? Why? Why not?

C5. What's the chance we are living in similar times today? Are we (the church) listening? Is there a call to repentance and holiness that we are not hearing?

D. DESTRUCTION

D1. Do you think that you can tell lost people the truth so often and so dramatically that rather than convince them to change you cause their hearts to become even more hardened – even to the point of no return?

Q. Do you think this hardening could have happened to Israel and Judah? What evidence can you think of that might support this concept?

D2. What foreign county invaded and exiled the Northern Kingdom, and what did God tell Judah in 10:24-25?
Isaiah 10:24-25   *Therefore thus says the Lord God of hosts: "O my people, who dwell in Zion, be not afraid of the Assyrians when they strike with the rod and lift up their staff against you as the Egyptians did. 25 For in a very little while my fury will come to an end, and my anger will be directed to their destruction."* ESV

D3. How do you explain the idea that God allowed Assyria to punish Israel (the Northern Kingdom), but then He punished or judged Assyria for that act?

E. RESTORATION

E1. What is the good news for the remnant in Isa 4:2-6?
Isaiah 4:2-6   *In that day the branch of the Lord shall be beautiful and glorious, and the fruit of the land shall be the pride and honor of the survivors of Israel. 3 And he who is left in Zion and remains in Jerusalem will be called holy, everyone who has been recorded for life in Jerusalem, 4 when the Lord shall have washed away the filth of the daughters of Zion and cleansed the bloodstains of Jerusalem from its midst by a spirit of judgment and by a spirit of burning. 5 Then the Lord will create over the whole site of Mount Zion and over her assemblies a cloud by day, and smoke and the shining of a flaming fire by night; for over all the glory there will be a canopy. 6*

There will be a booth for shade by day from the heat, and for a refuge and a shelter from the storm and rain. ESV

Q. What is the good news in Isa 31:6?
Isaiah 31:6   *Return to the One the Israelites have greatly rebelled against.*

E2. What did God promise in Isaiah 46:4, *even to your old age I am he, and to gray hairs I will carry you. I have made, and I will bear; I will carry and will save.* ESV

E3. In a nod to end times events 45:20 addresses the fugitives or survivors from the Gentile nations who turn to the Lord (45:22). What is their fate and why?
Isaiah 45:22   *Turn to me and be saved, all the ends of the earth! For I am God, and there is no other.* ESV

E4. Why is a remnant necessary?

F. APPLICATION

F1. What hope do you find personally in the promise of a remnant?

F2. Israel was accused of living in a state of unrepentance while committing injustice, unrighteousness, and unfaithfulness. Do those accusations have any application in your life, or in the life of your family or friends? How about co-workers or neighbors?

F3. Are you living or existing in a state of unreality? Are you hearing only the promises of Scripture and ignoring the conditions and warnings?

Transformation Road Map

Primary Takeaways

1: Even in the face of death, salvation is attainable through simple faith and a plea for remembrance, as demonstrated by the criminal on the cross who, despite his lack of works, rituals, or outward displays of faith, was promised paradise simply by acknowledging Jesus and asking to be remembered.

2: Angels are messengers and servants of God who play various roles in the divine plan, but they are not to be worshipped.

3: Overconfidence and disobedience can lead to defeat, as illustrated by Israel's victory at Jericho, followed by their defeat at Ai due to Achan's sin of taking devoted things.

4: When God assigns a task, He equips His people with both the skills and the desire to fulfill it, as demonstrated by the Israelites' divinely empowered craftsmanship and willing generosity in constructing the tabernacle.

5: Structured and divinely appointed worship leadership—combining prophetic music, thanksgiving, and generational continuity—creates a lasting legacy of praise that honors God's enduring covenant and mercy.

6: God appoints prophets as spiritual watchmen to hold leaders accountable as shepherds, warning that their failure to lead righteously results in societal collapse.

7: God's faithfulness to preserve a remnant of His people endures even through periods of judgment, serving as a testament to His covenant promises and ultimate plan for restoration.

Free PDF
MAKE WISE DECISIONS

[Get the ebook version for 99 cents]

Consequences Shape Lives.

This book discusses the nature of decisions and explores eight essential questions to make better decisions.

You are a few decisions away from transforming your life. You can make better decisions! This resource has sections on what makes a poor decision, questions to ask yourself, traps to avoid, short and sweet decisions, the wise decision framework, and twenty ways to be wise. It also has a handy decision-making checklist. (12 pages)

Free PDF: https://getwisdompublishing.com/resource-registration/

Kindle ebook for 99 cents: https://www.amazon.com/dp/B0FG8NC53J

Ebook

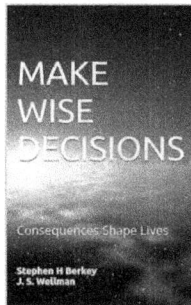

MAKE WISE DECISIONS

Consequences Shape Lives

Stephen H Berkey
J. S. Wellman

Free PDF

Ten Steps to Wise Choices

Timeless Wisdom. Practical Tools. Lasting Impact.

Free PDF
Life Improvement Principles
[Get the ebook version for 99 cents]

You can live your best life!

Welcome to a journey of discovery! In case you have forgotten, your actions have consequences. Unlock your potential! This book (60+ pages) provides the overview of all our strategies and wisdom principles to live your best life. You *can* transform your life! Get your wisdom-based roadmap to a better life and unlock all the possibilities for growth and success.

Free PDF: https://getwisdompublishing.com/resource-registration/

Kindle ebook for 99 cents:
https://www.amazon.com/dp/B0FG883KZM

Ebook

Life Improvement Principles

You can live your best life!

Stephen H Berkey
J. S. Wellman

Free PDF

Make it your life goal to be the best you can be!

Discover Wisdom and live the life you deserve.

Next Steps!

Continue Studying the *OBSCURE* Series
The *OBSCURE* Bible Study Series
https://www.amazon.com/dp/B08T7TL1B1

Be Challenged by the Jesus Follower Series
The Jesus Follower Bible Study Series
https://www.amazon.com/dp/B0DHP39P5J

Tackle Wisdom-Driven Life Change
Apply Biblical Wisdom to Live Your Best Life!
"Effective Life Change"
https://www.amazon.com/dp/1952359732

Know What You Should Pray
Personal Daily Prayer Guide
https://www.amazon.com/What-Should-Pray-Personal-Journal/dp/1952359260/

Decide to be the Very Best You Can Be
The Life Planning Series
https://www.amazon.com/dp/B09TH9SYC4

You Can Help:
SOCIAL MEDIA: Mention The *OBSCURE* Bible Study Series on your social platforms. Include the hashtag #obscurebiblestudy so we are aware of your post.

FRIENDS: Recommend *OBSCURE* to your family, friends, small group, Sunday School class leaders, or your church.

REVIEW: Please give us your honest review at
https://www.amazon.com/dp/195235918X

The *OBSCURE* Bible Study Series

**Continue your journey through the hidden
wisdom of Scripture with the OBSCURE Series.**

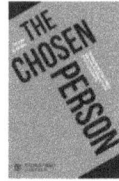

Blasphemy, Grace, Quarrels & Reconciliation: The lives of first-century disciples.
This book presents Joseph of Arimathea, Joanna, Ananias, Hymenaeus, and Cornelius (a centurion). It illustrates the nature and challenges of life as a first-century disciple.

The Beginning and the End: From creation to eternity.
This book has four lessons from Genesis and four from Revelation covering creation, rebellion, grace, worship, and eternity. God is leading us to worship in the Throne Room.

God at the Center: He is sovereign and I am not.
This book examines the virgin birth, worship, prayer, the sovereignty of God, compromise, and trust. God is at the center of all these stories. He is at the center of our lives.

Women of Courage: God did some serious business with these women.
This book examines the lives of Jael, Rizpah, the woman of Tekoa, Tabitha, Shiphrah, and Lydia. These women exhibit great courage and faithfulness. God used them in amazing ways.

The Beginning of Wisdom: Your personal character counts.
In this book we find courage, loyalty, thankfulness, love, forgiveness, and humility. Personal character counts. Decisions have consequences. Wisdom will help us stand firm in our faith.

Miracles & Rebellion: The good, the bad, and the indifferent.
God hates sin and loves to heal the faithful. The rebellion of Korah, Haman, and Alexander compare to the healing stories of Aeneas, a slave girl, and the crippled man at Lystra.

The Chosen People: There is a remnant.
This book concentrates mostly on Israel in the Old Testament, but also covers some interesting subjects as Lucifer, Michael the archangel, and Job's wife.

The Chosen Person: Keep your eyes on Jesus.
The focus is on Jesus and the superiority of Christ. We investigate Melchizedek, the disciples on the road to Emmaus, Nicodemus, and the criminal on the cross.

WEBSITE: http://getwisdompublishing.com/products/
AMAZON: www.amazon.com/author/stephenhberkey

Jesus Follower Bible Study Series

The Jesus Follower Bible Study Series will provide you with a complete description of the nature, characteristics, obligations, commitments, and responsibilities of a true Jesus follower.

Go to our Amazon Book Series page for your copy:

https://www.amazon.com/dp/B0DHP39P5J

The RELATIONSHIP CHARACTERISTICS of a Jesus Follower:
> Are you right with God?

The ONE ANOTHER INSTRUCTIONS to a Jesus Follower:
> Are you right with one another?

The WORSHIP of a Jesus Follower:
> Is your worship acceptable or in vain?

The PRAYER of a Jesus Follower:
> What Scripture says about unleashing the power of God.

The DANGERS of SIN for a Jesus Follower:
> God HATES sin! He abhors sin!

The FOCUS for a Jesus Follower:
> Keep your eyes fixed on Jesus!

The HEART Requirements of a Jesus Follower:
> Follow with all your heart, mind, body, and soul!

The COMMITMENTS of a Jesus Follower:
> Practical Christian living and discipleship.

The OBEDIENCE Requirements for a Jesus Follower:
> Ignore at your own risk!

"Get Wisdom Publishing creates wisdom-driven products that equip readers with timeless insights, understanding, and actionable tools to transform their lives."

Life Planning Series

Read these books if you want to live a better life.

The primary audience for this series is the secular self-help market, but the concepts are Christian based.

CHOOSE FAITH	**For the spiritual seeker and those with spiritual questions.** *Your Spiritual Guidebook For Questions About Religion, God, Heaven, Truth, Evil, and the Afterlife.* https://www.amazon.com/dp/1952359473
CHOOSE CORE VALUES	**Core values will drive your life.** https://www.amazon.com/dp/195235949X

Other Titles in the Life Planning Series
CHOOSE Integrity
CHOOSE Friends Wisely
CHOOSE The Right Words
CHOOSE Good Work Habits
CHOOSE Financial Responsibility
CHOOSE A Positive Self-Image
CHOOSE Leadership
CHOOSE Love and Family
LIFE PLANNING HANDBOOK A Life Plan Is The Key To Personal Growth https://www.amazon.com/gp/product/1952359325

Go to:

https://www.amazon.com/dp/B09TH9SYC4

to get these books.

Personal Daily Prayer Guide
Prayer Resource and Journal

This is a great resource to kick-start your prayer life!

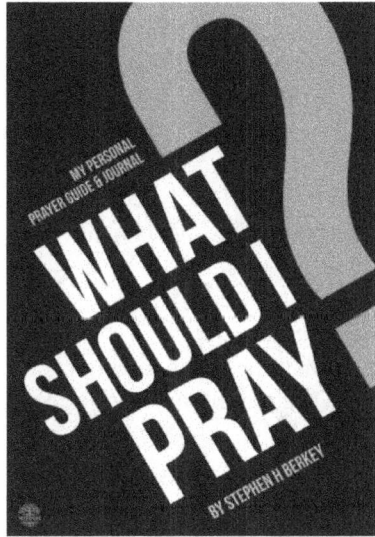

Know what to pray.
Pray based on Bible verses.
Strengthen your prayer life.
Access reference resources.
Pray with eternal implications.
Write your own prayers if desired.
Organize and focus your prayer time.
Learn what the Bible says about prayer.
Find encouragement and advice on how to pray.
Reduce frustration and distraction in your prayer time.

Get your copy today!

https://www.amazon.com/What-Should-Pray-Personal-Journal/dp/1952359260/

Acknowledgments

Arlene
Arlene has served as wife, editor, and proof-reader for all of my writing – thank you for your patience, help, and love.

Michelle
Michelle, our older daughter, has been an invaluable resource. She has graciously produced the website at www.getwisdompublishing.com. She was the first author in the family: graceandthegravelroad.com.

Stephanie
Our middle daughter designed all the covers for the *OBSCURE* Bible Study Series, as well as the marks and logos for Get Wisdom Publishing. We are grateful for her talent!

KOINONIA Small Group
These dear friends have hung in there with me as I taught many of the lessons to them first. Their input, answers, and suggestions have been invaluable.

God, Jesus, and Holy Spirit
Thank you, Lord, for Your guidance and direction.

Notes

1 Nelson's Illustrated Bible Dictionary, Copyright © 1986, Thomas Nelson Publishers; from PC Study Bible, "Archangel"
2 Nelson's Illustrated Bible Dictionary, Copyright © 1986, Thomas Nelson Publishers; from PC Study Bible, "Covetousness"
3 Nelson's Illustrated Bible Dictionary, Copyright © 1986, Thomas Nelson Publishers; from PC Study Bible, "Ark of the Covenant"

About the Author

Steve attended church as a child and accepted Christ when he was 10 years old. But his walk with Jesus left a lot to be desired for the next 44 years. In 1994 he "wrestled" with God for some period of months and in September of that year totally surrendered his life to Jesus.

In 1996 he was so driven to study God's Word that he attended the Indianapolis campus of Trinity Evangelical Divinity School (Chicago) to earn a Certificate of Biblical Studies. His hunger for God's Word led him to lead and write all his own Bible studies for his small group. He has been an entrepreneur and Bible study leader for the past 30 years.

He is a member of The Church at Station Hill in Spring Hill, TN, a regional campus of Brentwood Baptist (Brentwood TN).

GET**WISDOM**
PUBLISHING

www.getwisdompublishing.com

"Get Wisdom Publishing is dedicated to being the trusted source of wisdom-driven books that inspire growth, guide decisions, and empower readers to live with purpose and fulfillment."

Contact Us

Website: www.getwisdompublishing.com

Email: info@getwisdompublishing.com

Facebook: Get Wisdom Publishing

Author's Page: www.amazon.com/author/stephenhberkey

Amazon's Obscure Bible Study Series page:
https://www.amazon.com/dp/B08T7TL1B1

"Go beyond devotionals.
Experience biblical wisdom in action!"

www.ingramcontent.com/pod-product-compliance
Lightning Source LLC
Chambersburg PA
CBHW070813050426
42452CB00011B/2017